*GCSE PASSBOOK*

# SOCIOLOGY

## Stephen Moore

First published 1988
by Charles Letts & Co Ltd
Diary House, Borough Road, London SE1 1DW

Illustrations: Chartwell Illustrations

**British Library Cataloguing in Publication Data**
Moore, Stephen, *1950 –*
    Sociology. – (Key facts, GCSE passbooks).
    1. Sociology
    I. Title    II. Series
    301    HM66
ISBN 0 85097 807 6

Printed and bound in Great Britain by
Charles Letts (Scotland) Ltd

# Contents

# Acknowledgements

My grateful thanks to Keith Laker and Paola Moore for their assistance. I am also indebted to Hatti and Tuan of Solidisk Technology Ltd for word processing facilities.

The publishers are grateful to the following individuals and organizations for permission to publish copyright material which appears in illustrations within this book:

The Controller of Her Majesty's Stationery Office: p. 121, Central Statistical Office; pp. 18, 19, 21, 37, 38, 76, 100 from *Social Trends* (published by the Central Statistical Office); pp. 29, 30, 60, 61, 67, 69 Department of Employment; p. 78 Department of Education and Science; p. 123 Department of Health and Social Security;

Tony Garrett/*New Society*: pp. 25, 34, 45, 69, 86, 103, 113, 115;

*New Society*: pp. 55, 108, 129;

Gower/SCPR: p. 44, from *British Social Attitudes: The 1985 Report*;

University Grants Committee: p. 79;

Joint Industry Committee for National Readership Surveys: p. 118;

Nigel Paige: p. 138;

Heinemann Educational Books Ltd: p. 142, from *A Handbook for Sociology Teachers*, by Roger Gomm and Patrick McNeill.

## The organization of this book

This book contains full coverage of all the main areas of the
GCSE Sociology syllabuses examined in Britain. It also covers
large sections of the Social Science and Social Studies syllabuses
of all the British examination boards. It is written in the clearest
style possible, in order to give you a fast and comprehensive
understanding of Sociology.

The first section of the book is a brief outline of the aims and
requirements of the Sociology course which you are following.
This should enable you to prepare yourself for the examination
and your assessed coursework, by understanding just what the
examiners are looking for.

The next section gives advice on how to approach and take
examinations. It should be stressed that passing an examination
is not especially difficult if you are calm, have studied the
material and are well organized. You will find the book helpful in
all of these areas.

The third section of the book will suggest the very best way to
prepare a revision programme for your examination. If you follow
this you will ensure that you arrive at the examination feeling
confident and secure in your knowledge of the subject and your
ability to use it sensibly when asked questions.

There then follows the main section of this book, the subject
matter of Sociology. There is an important point I want you to
remember about this. Do not learn the material off by heart in
order to repeat it parrot-fashion in the examination. This is not
the point of the book, and you will not be able to answer the
questions in the examination. Think about the information and
arguments given in the book. Ask yourself:

1  Do I agree with the points raised?
2  Do they make sense, even if I disagree?
3  Why are they different from my ideas?
4  What are the implications of the information provided?
5  Could I make use of some of the information as starting points
for projects?

Use the information and ideas presented to you in this book. Let
it be your guide and friend, not a boss forcing you to do what it
wants.

Each chapter will begin with a brief outline of the contents. This will give you an idea of where each chapter is heading, so you do not get lost. At the end of each chapter there will be a set of questions. They are intended to make you reflect a little on the information given. There are some outline answers at the back of the book, just to make sure you are on the right lines.

Some of the information given in chapter 10 of this book, concerning British political parties, may be out of date. At the time of going to press, discussions were being held between the Liberal Party and the Social Democratic Party concerning plans to merge. You should consult your teacher for advice.

For most subjects examined at GCSE, National Criteria have been laid down – that is, areas of study that you must cover, and the knowledge, understanding and skills that you should have at the end of your course. However, a decision was taken that there should be no National Criteria for Sociology, even though it is one of the major examination subjects in Britain. Nevertheless, the examining boards have broadly agreed on the most important areas of study in Sociology. They also broadly agree on what the aims and objectives of a course in Sociology ought to be.

## The Aims

1 To promote an individual's awareness, knowledge and understanding of society and its development.
2 To give the individual some appreciation of the different ways of life in other societies.
3 To enhance an individual's ability to apply the knowledge learned to understanding his or her own life.
4 To encourage a critical awareness of social, political and economic arrangements and their effects in society.
5 To be able to understand and use sociological methods, including the collection, analysis and interpretation of data.

## Assessment

The examining boards have laid down how they will assess the student in terms of these aims. The student ought to demonstrate:
1 A knowledge and understanding of sociological topics.
2 A knowledge and understanding of sociological terms and concepts.
3 The ability to analyse and interpret evidence and data of various types.
4 The ability to evaluate evidence and distinguish between facts, values and opinions.
5 To select evidence and to present information in a coherent manner.
Throughout the book, points of special importance are denoted by use of the 'K' symbol.

It is most important that you devise a revision programme for yourself. This will ensure that you are fully prepared for the examination.

It is worth buying a large wall-chart type of Year Planner. You can then mark on it (a) when the examinations are, and (b) when your coursework assessment has to be in. This will allow you to work out how many weeks you have, and the pace at which you must move.

Next, divide the number of days/weeks by the number of subjects you are taking, so you know how many days you have for revising each one.

Write on each week/day the subjects you intend to study. You should allow some subjects a little longer, or less, than others, depending upon how easy you find them. If you are really well organized (as you will be in Sociology!) it is worth subdividing the weeks/days spent on a particular subject into topic areas. For instance, Sociology could be broken down by the chapter headings in this book.

Always study on your own and away from outside distractions. Having a stereo on gently in the background is one thing, but sitting in the living room with the television on is another!

Read each chapter through. Do not hurry. If you get tired, have a short break and then go back to work. Just reading the book without taking any information in is pointless.

If you do not understand something, read it over again. If you are really stuck, ask your teacher. This book is not meant to replace him/her, but to help you organize yourself better.

You bought this book; if you want to underline things, or use a marker pen, or write comments in it – then do so.

The GCE and the CSE examinations were concerned mainly with learning knowledge. This is still important, but you must also be able to **use** the knowledge in this book. As you go through it, you should try to see if you agree, or if some of the ideas remind you of experiences you have had. I have tried to avoid jargon and lots of names, but I have included different explanations for the same problem. Decide which one you think is best, and why you think so.

Link your study of Sociology with regular reading of a 'quality' newspaper like *The Independent, The Guardian, The Times* or *The Daily Telegraph.*

Answer the questions and check them against my suggestions. Remember that there are other answers than the ones I give. Often you will not be wrong if your reply is different from mine.

One good way of remembering things and thinking about them is to draw a diagram of some kind which summarizes what you have just learned. Try doing this at the end of each section in the book.

## Aims of the chapter

In this chapter we will examine:

**1** The way that behaviour is socially constructed, rather than being biological in origin.
**2** The wide variety of ways of living. British society is just one.
**3** Socialization, which is needed if people are to be more than just 'animals'.
**4** The nature of socialization and the most important agencies which help to socialize us.
**5** The meaning of culture and subculture, and how they are formed.
**6** Another society other than our own, to show how very differently other people can live.

### Socialization

In order for a society to exist, it is necessary to have some degree of agreement on values and on acceptable forms of behaviour. If people had nothing in common, they could not mix together without chaos occurring. **Socialization** is the process where people learn the patterns of behaviour considered normal in society.

*Instinct or learning?*
The behaviour of many animals can be explained by **biologically inherited drives**. What this means is that the way they act is born into them as a natural characteristic, over which they have no control. Birds know through biologically inherited characteristics that they must migrate at a certain time of year. Some people have suggested that biological drives are the explanation for human behaviour. However, sociologists say that, although we clearly have some biological drives, these are swamped by patterns of behaviour we learn from others. For example, the instinct of self-preservation may be overcome in certain circumstances, when people risk their own lives to save the lives of others, or when they commit suicide.

It has been suggested that the best proof of the sociological argument that our behaviour is the result of socialization, rather than biology, is the variation in behaviour which can be found over time and society. If behaviour was inherited biologically, then we would expect all human beings to have the same patterns of behaviour. This is not true; patterns of behaviour which are considered 'normal' vary widely, according to time and to society.

Examples of this include the expected patterns of behaviour of women:

**1 Over time** In Victorian England it was believed that women had no natural sexual drive. Today, it is accepted that women have the same sexual drive as men. Women were not thought capable of running businesses or of being politicians; today, they are considered as capable as any man.

**2 Across society** The mother instinct is considered quite normal in British society, and so it comes as a shock to find that some women show little interest in their children (although it is not commented on if fathers are not particularly interested).

However, in the Manus tribe of New Guinea, it was considered normal for the father to look after the child and, apart from bearing the child and breast-feeding it, women showed little interest in children. In the Ik tribe of Uganda, mothers showed absolutely no interest in their children and would happily abandon them if they were troublesome. In the Tchambuli tribe of the South Pacific, the women were the tough, forceful ones and the men were timid and would spend hours making themselves look beautiful.

*People without socialization*
People who have not been socialized have patterns of behaviour which are difficult to recognize as being human.

In the 1930s a girl called Anna, who was about five years old, was discovered on a farm in the United States. She had been completely isolated all her life, locked in a shed. This was because she was illegitimate and her grandparents were ashamed of her. When discovered, she had no idea how to talk, to walk, to control her bowels, to understand what was being said to her. She had no idea how to behave towards other people, and could only eat with her hands. So, people isolated from others are not able to act normally, according to society's expectations.

### The process of socialization

Socialization takes place mainly in childhood, but continues throughout our lives, as we learn behaviour and attitudes which are considered normal and appropriate for us. **Agencies of socialization** include the family, school, peer groups, the mass media and religion. Sociologists distinguish between two types of socialization – **primary** and **secondary**.

*Primary socialization*
This is the socialization that takes place between an individual

and the group with which he/she is in close contact, such as the family or the peer group (such as friends or classmates at school). It is from these that people first learn about how to behave.

**1 The family** This is probably the most important agency of socialization. Children identify with parents, copy them and do as they are told by them. The result is that children soon learn what is correct behaviour according to their parents, without being told. As the family is the first socializing agency, it is often the most important in people's lives. Girls and boys are socialized in quite different ways, to produce the different patterns of behaviour we associate with the sexes.

**2 The peer group** The second important influence on a child's life is that of the peer group. The peer group usually consists of friends, but it also includes all the people of roughly the same age whose behaviour influences you. Children play together, and later as youths they go around together. To be accepted by the group is very important to most people, and so they will modify their behaviour in order to seek approval.

*Secondary socialization*
Secondary socialization usually happens in more formal situations, which are not so personal – the two most important ones are the school and the mass media.

**1 Schools** Children from a wide variety of backgrounds attend schools, where they are taught a set of values and a form of knowledge considered important. As well as this formally taught knowledge (known as the **curriculum**), pupils also learn a whole set of hidden values and skills which exist in the school, and are often taken for granted by teachers. For example, the teachers may insist that no distinctions are made between boys and girls and all must have equal opportunities. However, in practice they may encourage male and female pupils to take different subjects, follow different careers, they may speak in different ways to males and females, etc. This hidden teaching of the school is called the **hidden curriculum** and is very important.

**2 The mass media** Apart from our direct experience, most of us learn about the world through the newspapers and television – the mass media. Attitudes and patterns of behaviour are influenced by the information given and the way it is presented. Attitudes towards other countries, ethnic groups, gender-appropriate behaviour and political events, for example, are all affected by the media treatment of them.

**3 Religion** This was once a most important agency of socialization, but it has declined in influence in recent years.

However, the basic values of British society are still those of the Christian churches.

## Variations in socialization

**1 Social class** Values and patterns of behaviour vary by social class. Middle-class people are likely to have different attitudes to politics, leisure and patterns of work, for example, than working-class people.

The Newsons studied child-rearing in Nottingham among the working and the middle classes. They found that the working class were stricter with their children, were more likely to discipline them and less likely to explain things to them.

**2 Ethnic group** Different cultural backgrounds are reflected in different upbringings. For example, the way a child of Asian background is brought up in Britain is likely to be different from the mainstream values of British society. Asian parents are much stricter and expect greater respect and obedience from their children. Girls are expected to be extremely modest and are not expected to talk to or be friendly with boys outside their family. The importance of the family and loyalty to it is stressed.

## Culture

**1 Culture** is the whole of the knowledge, ideas and habits of a society which are passed on from one generation to another. Culture is not static, but changes over time.

**2 Subcultures** are distinctive sets of values which exist within the mainstream culture. They are different to, but do not oppose, the main culture. The changing subcultures of youth are a good example of this.

**3 Contracultures** are distinctive sets of values that occur in a society, which challenge the main culture. The values of certain religious sects which reject the values of society are examples of this.

### The components of culture

**1 Beliefs** These are general, vague opinions about the world and the nature of society. They vary from one culture or subculture to another.

**2 Values** These are ideas about what is right or wrong in the world. They imply that certain forms of action ought to be taken. For example, life is precious, therefore one should not kill.

**3 Norms** These are socially expected patterns of behaviour.

They are clear guidelines on how people ought to behave in particular situations. When there are a number of people waiting to be served in a shop, they should form a queue.

**4 Roles** This is the pattern of behaviour that is associated with particular positions or occupations in society. Priests are expected to be pleasant, clean living, well spoken and helpful. A mother is supposed to be loving and concerned about her children.

**5 Role conflict** All of us play a number of roles in our lives. For me it is of teacher/writer/father/husband/friend/son, etc. Sometimes these roles come into conflict with each other. For example, being a good father and a writer are difficult to combine, as they both demand my time when not at work.

**6 Status** People are treated with different amounts of prestige in society. Certain positions receive more prestige than others. What position is regarded as high status varies by time and society. There are two forms of status: (a) when status is the result of a person's efforts, this is known as **achieved status** and (b) when status is the result of the position a person is born into, it is known as **ascribed status**.

*The culture of another society: the people of Samoa in the 1930s*
Samoa is a small island in the Pacific Ocean. It was studied in the late 1930s by Margaret Mead.

The Samoans lived from agriculture and fishing, inhabiting small villages composed of about 30 – 40 households. Each household was made up of a large number of relatives, some blood relations, some adopted.

Each household was headed by a Matai who was often the oldest male. The Matai of the village made all important decisions. Status and power in the villages was based solely upon age. The older the person, the greater the authority.

Family relationships were extremely important and any member of the family had a right to demand assistance of the others, no matter how great the demands he/she made. The most important values according to the Samoans were generosity and kindness. Those who did not show this were looked down upon.

Work was divided according to age and sex. Young women, for example, did a lot of the heavy manual work in agriculture such as weeding, gathering crops, etc. Fit adult men fished in the open sea – a dangerous task. Older men and women spun thread and fibre.

There were no official laws, nor was there any type of police or law system. Disputes were settled after discussion between the Matai. Ownership and wealth were not important.

## Summary

1  Our behaviour is a result of learning, not biological drives.
2  This process of learning the values and beliefs of society is known as **socialization**.
3  One can prove this by examining the wide variety of behaviour expected of women in different societies.
4  People who are are not socialized are more like animals than humans.
5  Socialization is divided into two: primary and secondary.
6  Within societies, people develop different subcultures.
7  Cultures are built up of specific beliefs, norms, values and roles.

## Revision questions

1  What is meant by **socialization**?
2  Give an example of someone who was not socialized. How did he or she behave? What does this show us concerning human actions?
3  Show how the family is involved in socialization.
4  How do schools unintentionally help in the socialization process?
5  What are subcultures? Give an example.
6  What are (a) roles, and (b) role conflicts? Give an example of each.
7  Take any one other society and describe its culture.
8  What is a **norm**? Give two examples of your own.

# 2  Family and marriage

## Aims of the chapter

In this chapter we will examine:

1  Family types in different cultures.
2  Marriage types in different cultures.
3  The state of family and marriage in Britain today – stressing the wide variety of family types that exist.
4  The changing relationships in the family – in particular, the relationships between (a) the parents and children (b) the husband and wife (c) the older generation and the family.

5  The way that industrialization has affected the family.
6  The arguments that suggest the family is good for society.
7  The arguments that suggest the family is bad for society.
8  The reasons for marriages breaking down, and the
consequences.
9  Family life in Japan.

### Family types in different cultures

**1  The extended family**  Three generations (grandparents –
grandchildren) who live together or close by. Usually family
members help each other.
**2  The nuclear family**  Two generations (parents – children) who
live together. Bonds with other relatives are usually weaker than
in the extended family.
   The type of family most common in a society depends upon how
great is the need for help. If a large family is useful (for example,
in harvesting crops) then the extended family is normal. In
modern British society, the nuclear family is common, but in
many other societies in the past, including most of Europe, the
extended family was normal.

### Marriage types in different cultures

**1  Monogamy**  This is the marriage of one man to one woman. It
is normal in Europe, for example.
**2  Polygyny**  This is the marriage of one man and two or more
women. It is common in many societies based on the Muslim
religion, such as Saudi Arabia or Senegal.
**3  Polyandry**  The marriage of one woman with two or more
men. This is not as common as the other two marriage types. It is
found in Tibet, for instance, where one woman may marry a
number of brothers. This keeps the population down, in a society
where there is little land available to cultivate.

### Marriage and the family in Britain today

The most important point to remember, about families and
marriage in Britain today, is the **variety** of lifestyles that exist
side by side.
**1  The decline of the typical 'breakfast-cereal family'**  The
typical idea of the family is of a husband and wife and their young
children. In fact only a minority of British households are like
this. The reasons for the decline include:
(a) A rapid increase in **divorce**, which breaks up the family.
(b) The decision by many people to live together without marrying.

18

**Fig. 1** People in households: by type of household and family in which they live

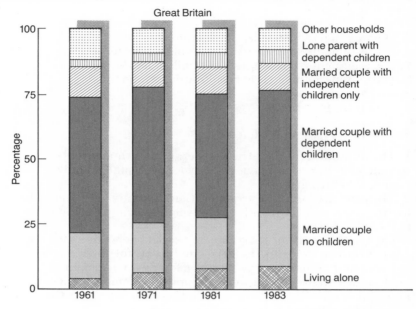

The 'typical' family of married couple with young (dependent) children is declining in number as a percentage of all households in Britain.

Source: *Social Trends,* 1986 (HMSO)

(c) The decision by many to delay or to reject having children. These people prefer to have a career and a high standard of living.
(d) The fact that there is a **life cycle** through which each family passes, as the children grow up and then leave home. At one point in time, there are relatively few families with young children, but still a large proportion of people are **going to** or **have had** children, but are in different stages of the family life cycle.
**2 The growth of single parent families** Today, about 9 per cent of households are a single parent and his/her children. These are increasing as a result of higher divorce rates, and because unmarried pregnant women no longer feel they have to marry the father of the child. This increase has been **criticized** by some people, who argue that children need both a mother and a father figure. They also argue that children suffer from the fact that either the parent goes out to work and leaves the child with a babyminder all day, or the parent does not work and so lives off state benefits, which means that the child is brought up in poverty.

In reply, it is argued that unhappily married parents create a dreadful atmosphere for children to be brought up in. Also, the level of state benefits for single parents ought to be increased to pull them out of poverty.

**Fig. 2** Marriage, remarriage and divorce                                                                19

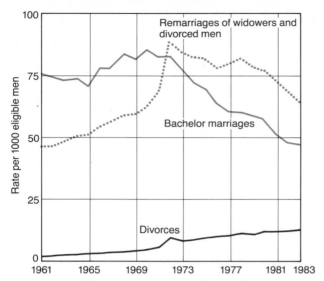

The graph shows the decline in first-time marriage and the slower decline in remarriages after 1970. Divorce continues to rise (although the rate has slowed down since 1983).

Source: *Social Trends,* 1986 (HMSO)

**3  Reconstituted families**  The growth in divorce has led to people with dependent children remarrying. This means that the children of two sets of parents are fused together into one large family, which can lead to tension and personal problems.

**4  The growth of cohabitation**  People are increasingly 'living together', rather than marrying. Today, of all couples marrying, two thirds have lived together.

This has been seen as a threat to marriage, although it is important to note that the vast majority of people do eventually marry. Almost 90 per cent of people marry (even if they later divorce) at some period in their lives. Most people who cohabit do so either before marriage, or in between ending one marriage and their remarriage to the person they are living with.

**5  Ethnic minority families**  These are often different in their form and style of life from the traditional British family. The growth in the number of people from different ethnic backgrounds in Britain has meant that alternative attitudes to marriage have been brought here.

*An example: Asian attitudes to marriage*
Many Asian marriages are still 'arranged'. The parents of the young people get together and decide on the marriage, and in

some cases the bride and bridegroom do not even meet before the marriage. Usually, though, they are allowed to meet and get to know each other well before the marriage.

Whereas the attitude towards women has changed greatly in the last 20 years amongst the majority of the population, the Asian communities believe that women ought to accept that the man is the head of the household and that they must obey his decisions. Women are not encouraged to go out, and certainly they cannot go to social occasions where there may be other men, without their husbands. They are expected to be very quiet and obedient, and 'correct' in their behaviour.

### Relationships in the family

In the last 100 years there have been a number of changes in the way that family members treat one another.

#### The husband – wife relationship

Traditionally, the husband was seen as the head of the family; the wife was less important. Amongst some of the working class, there was a belief that marriage was really a swap between a husband who provided the income from his job, and the wife who looked after the home and children.

By the 1950s it had become clear that there was a change in the attitudes of middle-class people. Husbands and wives were on far more of an equal footing, and they shared much of their leisure time, especially in gardening and DIY activities.

In the 1960s, research amongst car-assembly workers showed that this change in attitude was occurring amongst the working class too. The term **symmetrical family** was used. This meant that husband and wife shared equally in decision-making and in the activities of the home. The sharp division between the activities performed by the husband (the husband's role) and those by the wife (the wife's role) were broken down.

The reasons for the changing relationship were seen as:

**1** The breakdown of the working-class extended family. Now the husband and wife were forced to rely on each other.

**2** The changing attitudes of women towards their role, and the acceptance by the majority of husbands of this.

**3** The increasing importance of home ownership and the fact that couples were becoming more 'home-centred'.

**The feminist view of the husband – wife relationship** The idea that husbands and wives are equal in the family has been criticized by many sociologists, who argue that:

**1** Wives are still expected to do the majority of the housework.

2 Wives are still expected to give up or interrupt their careers for the children.
3 In most households, there are still jobs which the men do and jobs the women do.
4 'Housewives' work long hours for no financial reward and are treated as if they did not work at all.

**Fig. 3** Who does what in British families

| | Married people | | |
| --- | --- | --- | --- |
| | Mainly man | Mainly woman | Shared equally |
| **Household tasks** (percentage) | | | |
| Washing and ironing | 1 | 88 | 9 |
| Preparation of evening meal | 5 | 77 | 16 |
| Household cleaning | 3 | 72 | 23 |
| Household shopping | 6 | 54 | 39 |
| Evening dishes | 18 | 37 | 41 |
| Organization of household money and bills | 32 | 38 | 28 |
| Repairs of household equipment | 83 | 6 | 8 |
| | | | |
| **Child rearing** (percentage) | | | |
| Looks after the children when they are sick | 1 | 63 | 35 |
| Teaches the children discipline | 10 | 12 | 77 |

There is still a long way to go before the 'symmetrical family' becomes the reality in Britain.

Source: Gower/SCPR, 1985

*Parents and children*

Traditionally, children were treated as if they were not important and as if their views were not worth listening to. They had to obey their parents and remained very much under their control. Today, children are seen as very important by their parents and are treated as individuals. To some degree their opinion is asked and the family is a much more democratic unit. Control over children is much more relaxed, although the authority of the parents is still very real.

The reasons for the change include:
1 The greater stress on care and love for children in society,

rather than on obedience and discipline.

2  The smaller size of families, which means that children can be treated as individuals and loved in their own right. Large families meant great stress for parents.

3  The development of youth culture, which has meant that young people have demanded and won greater freedom and independence.

There are, however, **gender differences** in upbringing – parents treat sons and daughters differently, in that they encourage certain forms of behaviour amongst boys, and different behaviour amongst girls. They (a) give them different toys, (b) speak differently to them, (c) play different games with them and (d) are more protective and stricter with girls than boys.

### *The older generation and the family*

There has been a large increase in the expectation of life for most people. Today, for the first time in history, it is quite common for people to have grandparents right through to adulthood.

The fact is that most elderly people are neither isolated nor lonely. Only about a third of the over 65s live alone, and a half of the elderly receive a visit from a relative at least once a week. Only 2 per cent of the elderly live in residential homes. Where the younger generation live far away from their relatives, contact is maintained through telephone and letters.

However, the idea that grandparents are 'heads of the family' or that they have any real authority is no longer true.

## Industrialization and the changing form of the family

### *The situation before the Industrial Revolution*

In most of Europe it appears that the extended family was normal before the Industrial Revolution. However, in Britain evidence suggests that only 10 per cent of families were extended; about the same proportion as now. Nevertheless, there were large households. Better-off families would normally take in the children of the poorer people. These children would be treated almost as if they were the sons and daughters of the well-off families, but would be expected to help around the house and in the business. The result was that a lot of people lived in the better-off households.

It was rare for people to live long enough to be grandparents, as they married late, had children fairly late in life and then died young.

*The period from 1850 – 1950*
Amongst the working class it seems that industrialization actually created the extended family. As people moved into the towns and found work, they found that if a large group lived near each other, they could help each other to achieve a better standard of living. People began to live longer at this period and far fewer babies died at birth. The result was larger families and grandparents alive and able to care for children while the parents were at work.

So working-class communities developed in the big cities as families expanded and became extended, and then the extended families overlapped through marriage and friendship.

*The period 1955 onwards*
In this period the extended family began to decline. This was because the working class began to move out of the inner-city areas into new housing. Rising standards of living meant that the extended family with all its constraints was no longer needed. Couples could live well by themselves, so people moved in search of work and so lost daily contact with other members of the extended family.

The result was the **nuclear family** with its stress on close bonds between parents and children. The members of the nuclear family, however, are not cut off from other family members. The use of telephone, cars, trains, etc. allows people to keep fairly close contact over a wide distance.

The purposes of the family

*The positive approach*
Throughout history the family has been a useful means for people to give and receive mutual assistance. Before the rise in the standard of living and the introduction of the welfare state, the family ensured that most people in Britain had help if it was needed. Before industrialization, when most people were farmers, the whole family worked together as an economic unit to produce enough food to survive. Today, the situation is different but it is claimed that the family still performs useful functions both for society and for individual family members.

The functions of the family today include:
1 Regulation of sexual behaviour: sexual behaviour is generally expected to be restricted to husbands and wives. This limits possible conflicts and rivalries.
2 The family is the unit that ensures that society continues, by

producing the next generation.

**3** Socialization: children are socialized into the basic values and ideas of society through the family.

**4** Economic unit: the family does not work to produce goods, or farm together any longer; however, people still buy most things (houses, cars, audio equipment) in family units.

**5** Emotional support: the family is the unit which provides the emotional stability and support that most people need.

**K** ▶

### *The negative approach*

Not everyone agrees that the family benefits people and society.

**1** Emotionally intense: the family is so close that people can feel trapped. Tension and conflict follow.

**2** Women are repressed: it is women who do most of the domestic work and who have to give up careers to look after children. Those who stay at home as housewives work long hours, shut indoors with no company except for that of young children.

**3** Family violence: violence against wives and by parents on children is not uncommon. This is a result, largely, of the first two points.

## Marriage breakdown

There was a steady rise in divorce throughout this century, then in 1969 a law was passed which made it a lot easier to get divorced. Since then, the number of divorces has risen markedly.

**K** ▶

### *Reasons for the increase in divorce include*:

**1 Expectations of marriage** People have very high expectations of marriage today, as people marry 'for love'. In the past there was greater stress on the idea of partnership in marriage and expectations were much lower. The idea of being in love was not as important.

**2 Changing attitudes of women** Women are no longer content to accept an unhappy marriage. If they feel that they are being treated unfairly then they will divorce. Two thirds of divorces are started by women.

**3 Cultural and religious changes** The idea that it is immoral or wrong to divorce has declined with the diminishing power of religion. Today, most people see marriage as a private matter between individuals, not a religious act in the eyes of God. They are, therefore, less likely to continue to stay married if they feel unhappy.

**4 Legal changes** Throughout this century, changing attitudes have led to a softening of the laws on divorce. At the beginning of the century it was almost impossible for an ordinary person to obtain a divorce, no matter how bad the situation between the partners. Today, it is relatively easy.

**Fig. 4** The increase in divorce since 1961

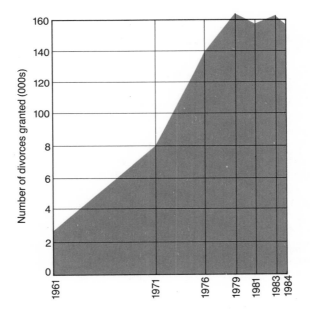

Source: *New Society*

*The continuing strength of marriage*
The fact that the numbers of people divorcing and cohabiting have increased greatly in the last twenty years has led some people to claim that marriage is under threat. However, arguments against this include the facts that divorce rates are now a more accurate picture of unhappy marriages, whereas in the past people could not obtain divorces, and that most divorcees remarry.

Family life in Japan: a comparison

1  The family in Japan is still of the extended type.
2  The father is the undisputed head of the household.
3  The relationship between husband and wife is an unequal one

in which the man is seen as having greater authority than the woman.

**4**  The wife is expected to do the majority of the housework. Children are treated strictly. They are forced to work hard at school.

**5**  The grandparents are still treated with considerable respect.

**6**  The family is still an important and respected institution.

## Summary

**1**  Types of family and types of marriage vary in different cultures. There is no 'normal' family or marriage type.

**2**  The nature of the family has changed considerably in modern Britain. The typical **nuclear family** is only one of a number of types which exist.

**3**  The relationships between husband and wife have changed considerably and there has been a move towards great equality.

**4**  However, women are still expected to undertake the majority of household tasks.

**5**  Children are now regarded as more important and their views are listened to.

**6**  Industrialization initially influenced the family by changing it from the nuclear type to the extended type. In the last 50 years there has been a move back towards the nuclear family.

**7**  One group of sociologists argue that the family is good for society and for family members.

**8**  Other sociologists argue that the family is harmful to its members, particularly women. Feminist sociologists have been particularly linked to this view.

**9**  There has been a very large rise in divorce rates in the last 30 years. This has led to the argument that marriage is less important than in the past.

## Revision questions

**1**  Explain the growth of single-parent families.

**2**  Give an example of family life amongst any ethnic minority in Britain.

**3**  In what ways has the relationship between husband and wife altered this century?

**4**  Was the typical family extended or nuclear, in Britain, before

the Industrial Revolution?
5  Why has the family been criticized as being 'bad' for people?
6  Give three reasons for the increase in the divorce rate.
7  Look at Fig. 1. Did the number of married couples with dependent children increase or decrease between 1961 and 1981?
8  Look at Fig. 2. Describe and explain the change in the remarriage rate.
9  Look at Fig. 3. What comment can you make on the statement that the typical family in Britain today is 'symmetrical'?

# 3 Work

## Aims of the chapter

In this chapter we will examine:

1  Exactly what the meaning of work is and how it differs from leisure.
2  A comparison of work today with work in a pre-industrial society.
3  The reasons for people going out to work.
4  How the occupational structure has changed in the last 20 years.
5  The importance of automation for workers and for society.
6  The meaning of alienation and its importance.
7  What makes work satisfying.
8  Why there are strikes.
9  What trade unions and professions do.
10  The influence of work on our lives outside the workplace.

### The meaning of work

There are very few actions which can be considered 'work' in themselves. 'Work' is a matter of definition. For example, playing tennis is a hobby for many of us, but work for tennis professionals.
    Work has the following elements:
1  It is paid.
2  It is not usually done for pleasure.
3  The employee accepts the authority of the person paying.

**4** Work time is clearly marked off from non-work time.
**5** It is usually done to produce something of value.

The division between work and non-work time is a modern idea. Before industrialization most people did not distinguish work from other respects of their lives. Work and leisure were totally integrated. The idea of employment too is a new idea.

The clear-cut division between work and leisure developed with the growth of factories. Machinery, located in factories, needed to be stopped and started at precise times. Workers, therefore, had to go into factories and work for set periods. Before the Industrial Revolution, most production was carried out at home and the whole family 'worked' together.

### Why people work

**1** For the wage – at first this seems the only reason, yet sociologists have shown that for most people, money is only part of the reason for working.
**2** For the enjoyment and satisfaction – this is true mainly for those doing skilled work.
**3** For companionship – people get company and friends at work.
**4** For a sense of identity and status – people are given a sense of who they are by their job, and a sense of importance.

### The occupational structure

There are two forms of labour:
**1 Manual work** This involves physical effort, such as working machinery and bricklaying.
**2 Non-manual labour** This relies far less on physical effort and more on mental effort or personality, for example, teaching and clerical work.

There are three types of industry:
**1 Primary** – these are industries which exploit natural resources, for example, agriculture and mining.
**2 Manufacturing** – these are industries which make things, for example, engineering and car production.
**3 Service** – these are industries which provide services of various kinds for people, for example, banking and leisure services.

### Change in the occupational structure

The following changes have taken place in the occupational structure of Britain:

**Fig. 1** The occupational structure of Britain

29

Who's doing what . . .

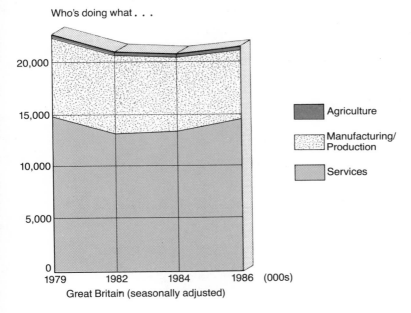

Agriculture

Manufacturing/ Production

Services

1979    1982    1984    1986    (000s)

Great Britain (seasonally adjusted)

Source: *Department of Employment*, 1986 (HMSO)

**1 A move away from manual work to non-manual work** Fewer people today are employed in manual jobs, and over half the workforce are now in non-manual jobs.

**2 A move away from primary and manufacturing industries towards service industries** Agriculture and manufacturing employ fewer and fewer people. On the other hand, there has been a growth in jobs in service industries (fig. 2).

**3 An increasing number of women workers** Alongside the changes mentioned earlier, there has been a large growth in the numbers of women in employment. This is in response to the growth in service industries, which employ a high proportion of women. Many women are only employed part-time, however.

**4 Growth in unemployment** One of the most noticeable things in the economy is the growth in the number of the unemployed. This is related to the decline of Britain as a manufacturing nation.

**5 The growth of the multi-nationals** Britain is unique in the world in the extent that so much employment is dominated by relatively few large firms. These are usually massive 'multi-nationals' which have companies in many different countries, for example, Ford Motor Company. Most other countries have far more medium-sized firms.

**Fig. 2** The decline in manufacturing 1971-85

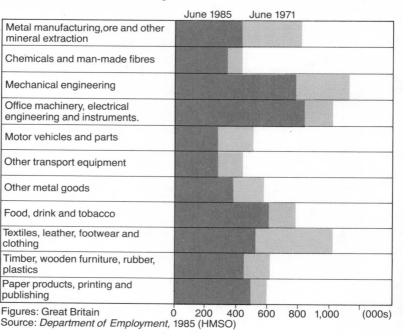

| | June 1985 | June 1971 |
|---|---|---|
| Metal manufacturing, ore and other mineral extraction | | |
| Chemicals and man-made fibres | | |
| Mechanical engineering | | |
| Office machinery, electrical engineering and instruments. | | |
| Motor vehicles and parts | | |
| Other transport equipment | | |
| Other metal goods | | |
| Food, drink and tobacco | | |
| Textiles, leather, footwear and clothing | | |
| Timber, wooden furniture, rubber, plastics | | |
| Paper products, printing and publishing | | |

Figures: Great Britain      0   200   400   600   800   1,000    (000s)
Source: *Department of Employment,* 1985 (HMSO)

## Manufacturing and the division of labour

Britain is an **industrialized** nation, which means that:
1 The production of articles is done in factories by large scale machinery.
2 The work is done by salaried employees.
3 The majority of people live in towns and cities.
4 A further characteristic of an industrialized society is the division of labour: this means that most people do not make complete articles, but only parts of articles. People in factories therefore constantly repeat the same action, for example, on a car production line each worker has a different task. It could be fitting the windscreen to each car – and that is the only task the person does. This means that articles are produced at low prices, because the system is very efficient, but it has the disadvantages that workers are bored and find their work unsatisfying. This can lead to strikes and absenteeism.

## Automation

**Automation** means that machinery performs complete processes without the need of workers to supervise. Increasingly it involves control of the work process by computers. Originally automation replaced unskilled work, but increasingly as computers become more sophisticated it is replacing highly skilled work, such as welding car bodies.

The advantages of automation for society include:
1 Boring and dangerous jobs can be replaced.
2 The quality of goods is improved as the machinery never varies in its work standard.
3 Some articles can be produced for a lower price.
4 As work is made easier and faster by computer, employees could eventually work shorter hours and have more leisure time.

The disadvantages of automation are:
1 The main disadvantage of automation for the worker is its main advantage to the employer – it is cheaper than an employee and so replaces him/her. The result is the possibility of greatly increased **unemployment**.
2 Automated machinery will take the skill out of a job and with it goes pride and interest.

*The wider consequences of automation*

**Fig. 3** Weighing up the advantages and disadvantages of automation

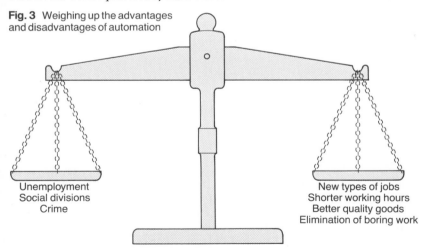

Unemployment
Social divisions
Crime

New types of jobs
Shorter working hours
Better quality goods
Elimination of boring work

Apart from the immediate advantages and disadvantages of automation, there are longer-term consequences for society:
1 Increasing unemployment might lead to wider social tensions such as crime, poverty and social unrest.
2 There would be a great divide between those in employment, who will have a decent standard of living, and the large numbers of unemployed.

**3** There may be political unrest as a result of this divide.
**4** As automation and better means of communication allow people to work and even shop from home, there will be a decline in the amount of contact people will have with each other and there may be a move towards isolation.
**5** If adequate standards of living are enjoyed by most people, employed or not, then a new form of society may develop based on leisure activities and self-development. However, this will depend on how wealth is distributed.

### Work satisfaction

For many people, work is boring and uninteresting. Marx called this situation **alienation**. It has the following elements:
**1** The worker feels that he/she is not using his/her full abilities.
**2** The worker feels he/she has no power over the work process – it is in the hands of the employers.
**3** The worker feels no pride and enjoyment in his/her job.
**4** The worker feels cut off from other people, in competition with them rather than as a member of a 'team'.

Alienation increases when:
**1** The worker does only a very small part of the whole production process.
**2** The task is constantly repeated.
**3** The job is boring.
**4** Little skill is needed.
**5** Workers have no control over their work.

Alienation decreases and work satisfaction is gained when:
**1** Employers create a pleasant work environment, which is comfortable and quiet.
**2** Employers give good welfare provision such as clubs, canteens, etc. (When employers do 1 and 2, it is known as the **human relations approach** to management.)
**3** The workers have some power in the work place – possibly through share-ownership schemes.
**4** There are no rigid divisions between workers and management.
**5** Workers do not do just one small part of the work process, but the whole job from start to finish.

In their daily lives at work, employees have 'strategies' which help them to cope with boring work and pass the day.
**1** Workers can limit output and do only what they consider to be a 'reasonable' amount of work.
**2** People can pass much of their time 'daydreaming' at work.

3  They play practical jokes and tricks on one another.
4  They may take unauthorized breaks.

## Industrial disputes

*Types of industrial action*
Striking is not the only form of pressure which workers can
impose upon management. The range of industrial actions
includes:
1  **Working to rule**  This means rigidly sticking to rules, which
effectively means slowing down.
2  **Industrial sabotage**  This means deliberately breaking
machinery – it is relatively rare, but does happen.

*Factors influencing the amount of strike action*
1  **Government action**  The Conservative Government in the
early 1980s passed a number of laws which strictly limited the
power of trade unions to call strikes. This has limited the number
of strikes. Employers can sack workers on unofficial strike.
2  **The state of the economy**  When there are few jobs available
and employers are able to hire other workers to replace those on
strike, then the number of strikes declines. Since the early 1980s,
this has been the situation in Britain.
3  However, workers still go on strike in order to get wage
increases and to gain or defend improvements at work.
4  Boring, routine work frustrates workers, who are more likely
to go on strike than people in interesting jobs.

## Trade unions

Trade unions are democratic organizations set up to represent the
interests of employees in negotiations with employers over such
things as pay, working conditions, holidays and safety matters.

*Organization*
Unions have permanent staff in headquarters, but also have
representatives in factories and offices who are elected by union
members in those places, In factories, these men are known as
'shop stewards'.

*Changes in unions*
Unions are losing members at a significant rate. It is claimed that
in the early 1980s more than two million members were lost. The

**Fig. 4** Who belongs to trade unions

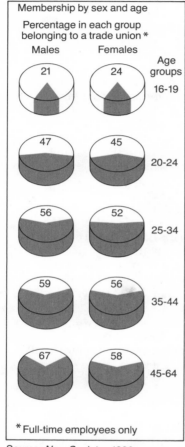

Membership by sex and age

Percentage in each group belonging to a trade union *

Males    Females    Age groups

21    24    16-19

47    45    20-24

56    52    25-34

59    56    35-44

67    58    45-64

* Full-time employees only

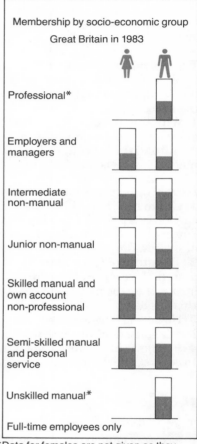

Membership by socio-economic group

Great Britain in 1983

Professional*

Employers and managers

Intermediate non-manual

Junior non-manual

Skilled manual and own account non-professional

Semi-skilled manual and personal service

Unskilled manual*

Full-time employees only

Source: *New Society*, 1986

*Data for females are not given as they relate only to a small number of employees.

decline is mainly because of unemployment and the general decline in manufacturing industry. The area of growth in trade-union membership is in offices, shops and in managerial staff. This is because more and more people are now employed in non-manual jobs and they are determined to win better conditions for themselves.

### K ▶ Professions

These are associations formed by certain groups performing some

of the highest rewarded jobs – such as doctors, solicitors, etc.
There are two views on professions:
1 They are there to maintain the highest standards of
professional practice and to benefit the clients or patients. They
are given great freedom by the Government to impose high
standards on new entrants and to maintain those standards.
2 The alternative view is that they are a form of middle-class
trade union and that they create an impression of how difficult
their work is in order to win high status and income for
themselves. Professionalization, according to this view, is seen as
an 'occupational strategy' to benefit themselves.
Sociologists have supported this second view.

## Work in another society: a comparative approach

In simple, pre-industrial societies such as were found in the
islands of the South Pacific up to 60 years ago, work was very
different.
1 There was no clear distinction between work and leisure, both
were woven together into a harmonious form of life. People
performed the tasks necessary to live, and helped each other.
2 Jobs were not necessarily done on ability, but on who
traditionally performed that job. If a person's father had done
something, for example, then the son would expect to inherit that
job.
3 The idea that there was a special time for working did not
exist. 'Work' was done when it needed to be done.
4 There was no special place put aside for work.

## The influence of work on our non-working lives

Work influences our life in many ways:
1 **Family life** is influenced by occupation: how many hours away
from home the person is, how tired he/she is after work, for
example.
2 **The community** is affected by work: close working-class
communities were created by the mines and factories of the last
century which would dominate small towns.
3 **Leisure** and spending patterns are linked to work: the more
money, the wider the leisure patterns and the higher the level of
purchase.
4 **Health** is related to work: some jobs are more dangerous than
others and there is a close relationship between types of illness
and occupation.

## Summary

1  What we know as 'work' is a modern idea which is very different from the way people obtained a living in the past.

2  People do not work solely for money, they also look for status and satisfaction.

3  The occupational structure of Britain has changed considerably this century. In recent years, there has been a major shift from manufacturing to service industries.

4  There has been an increase in the number of women working.

5  One of the most important changes in recent years has been the introduction of automation.

6  This has many social consequences. The best one is the possibility of having machines do all the worst jobs. The worst ones are the growth in unemployment and the possibility of friction between the unemployed and the employed.

7  Many people are alienated from their work. Usually they are performing boring, repetitive tasks.

8  Alienation makes workers more likely to strike and to show little interest in the quality of the product they are making.

9  There are a number of ways in which workers combat alienation – particularly daydreaming and 'messing about' in the workplace.

10  Strikes in Britain have declined in recent years because of the high unemployment rate and Government action.

11  Workers organize themselves in order to improve their pay and conditions. The working class have trade unions, while the middle class form professions.

12  Work influences our non-work lives in many ways, including family, health, leisure and community.

## Revision questions

1  What are the characteristics of work?

2  Do people only work for money?

3  Briefly describe the changes in the occupational structure in Britain.

4  What differences are there between an industrialized country and a non-industrialized one?

5  What are the possible consequences of automation?

6  What sort of work causes alienation?

7  What factors influence the level of strikes?

8  Are there any differences between trade unions and professions?

9  Compare work in Britain with work in a non-industrialized society.

10 Explain, with examples, how work can influence our wider lives.
11 Look at fig. 1. How many people were employed in service industry jobs in 1986?
12 Look at fig. 4. Which group of males had the highest membership of trade unions?

# 4 Unemployment

## Aims of the chapter

In this chapter we will examine:

1 The causes of unemployment in Britain.
2 Why some groups are more likely to become unemployed than others.
3 The consequences for the lives of the unemployed.
4 The relationship between unemployment and regions in Britain.
5 The implications, for society as a whole, of large-scale unemployment.

In the last 12 years there has been a great rise in the level of unemployment:

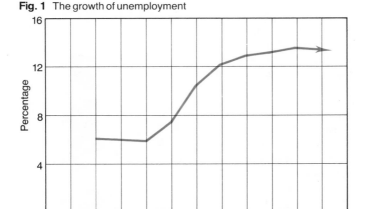

**Fig. 1** The growth of unemployment

Source: (adapted) *Social Trends,* 1986 (HMSO)

### K ▶ The causes of unemployment

**1** The decline of Britain as a manufacturing nation. Britain now imports more articles from other countries than it sells abroad. The economy of the country has largely rested on North Sea oil exports since 1979.
**2** The competition from newer industrialized nations where wage rates are lower and where working conditions are poorer.
**3** The development of automation in industry: automated machinery has replaced the jobs of many workers.
**4** Economic restructuring to make British industry competitive with foreign industries.

### K ▶ Groups most likely to experience unemployment

**1 The young** Those people who have little experience or qualifications to offer employers are not likely to gain employment, apart from on special Government schemes such as YTS.
**2 The old** Older workers, over 50, whom employers feel are not worth retraining, are most likely to be laid off. This group has the least likelihood of getting work.
**3 The ethnic minorities**
The unemployment rate for some of the ethnic minority groups is twice the national average. This is because some employers are thought to discriminate against them, preferring White workers, and because the ethnic minorities have a higher proportion of young people. We already know that young people of all backgrounds have higher rates of unemployment anyway.
**4 The least educated and least skilled** Three quarters of the unemployed are registered for manual work of one kind or another. With the decline in manufacturing and the increase in automation, there are fewer manual jobs.

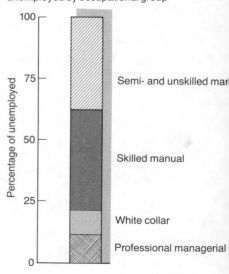

**Fig. 2** The composition of the unemployed by occupational group

Percentage of unemployed

Semi- and unskilled manual

Skilled manual

White collar

Professional managerial

Source: (adapted)
*Social Trends,* 1986 (HMSO)

5 **Those living in certain areas** Some areas have much higher rates of employment than others (see the next section).

## Unemployment by region

Not all areas of Britain have the same levels of unemployment. The north of Britain has the highest rates (apart from Northern Ireland). The lowest rates are in the south-east and East Anglia.

**Fig. 3** Unemployment by region

The reasons for variations in unemployment by region are:
1 The industries with the greatest levels of decline such as 'heavy' industries are in the north.

**2** The newer industries have developed in the south-east.
**3** The south-east is nearer Europe, and, therefore, the other countries of the EEC, which are now our most important trading partners.
**4** The only section of the economy which has not experienced decline is the service sector providing the range of services from banking and finance through to leisure activities. Banking has always been linked to the City of London, and the new leisure and services are drawn to areas where there is a degree of affluence. These are, therefore, attracted to the south-east and do not develop as well in the north.

## The implications of unemployment for society

Large numbers of people without work can have some very important consequences for society.
**1** Instead of Government spending going towards new projects such as hospitals or education, more money has to be spent on social security payments.
**2** Trade unions are weakened; employers can threaten workers with unemployment, as there is a large pool of the unemployed willing to work. This means a lowering of wages and working conditions.
**3** Some of the unemployed may turn to crime.
**4** There will be a division in society between the employed and the unemployed and this could cause political and social tensions. These sorts of division could undermine democracy, as in German and Italy in the earlier part of this century.

## How different groups experience unemployment

**1 The young** Young people have little experience or habit of work and, therefore, unemployment does not threaten their identities as we see happen with older people. Young people, however, may feel that they have little future and that they are unable to buy the objects (clothes and cars, for example) they have come to expect, and this can move them to crime.
**2 Middle-aged** People who have worked for a number of years identify with their jobs. Unemployment means a loss of identity. The fall in income hits the middle-aged particularly strongly, as they cannot maintain their standard of living. People feel failures. There appears to be a link between illness and unemployment amongst this age group.
**3 Women** Women have not been as badly hit by unemployment as men. This is because they are often in part-time work and are

so lowly paid that employers want to keep them. If they are unemployed, the independence of women is threatened if they have to return to accepting their husband's salary as the only family income. Official statistics of unemployment are thought to underestimate the number of unemployed women, as the way the statistics are collected excludes many women.

## Summary

1 There has been a great rise in unemployment in recent years.
2 Unemployment has been caused by the decline of Britain as a manufacturing nation, automation and restructuring.
3 Certain groups, particularly the young, older workers and the ethnic minorities, are more likely to be unemployed.
4 The north of Britain has been hardest hit by unemployment.
5 Unemployment has a number of important consequences for society, including a rise in social problems and a division in society between the employed and unemployed.
6 Unemployment hits different groups such as the young, the older workers, females and males in different ways.

## Revision questions

1 What causes have been suggested for unemployment?
2 Name three groups most likely to be or to become unemployed.
3 Why are there higher rates of unemployment amongst the ethnic minorities?
4 Why does the north have higher rates of unemployment than the south?
5 Suggest two implications for society of continuing high rates of unemployment.
6 Compare the reactions of young people and older people to unemployment.
7 Look at fig. 2. What percentages of the unemployed are from semi-skilled and unskilled backgrounds?
8 Look at fig. 3. Which area in England has the highest level of unemployment?

# 5 Social stratification

## Aims of the chapter

In this chapter we will examine:

1 The different forms of stratification.
2 The ways in which social class influences a person's life.
3 How sociologists measure social class.
4 The ways in which, overall, the class structure of Britain has changed in the last 35 years.
5 The specific changes in the working class.
6 The specific changes in the middle class.
7 The explanations of Karl Marx and Max Weber for social class.
8 What social mobility is, and what the causes are.
9 The distribution of wealth and income amongst the population.

In virtually all societies, people are aware of divisions between various groups, and as a result of these divisions people are treated differently. Sociologists usually call these divisions strata, so the division of people into groups is known as social stratification. In British society today, the most important divisions are those of sex, ethnic group (which people generally recognize by skin colour) age and social class.

In this chapter we are going to examine social class. The differences based on sex, age and ethnic group will be examined in following units.

## Different forms of stratification in history

### Slavery

In Ancient Greece and Rome, society was divided into two groups – the free people and the slaves. Slaves were people who were owned by others and could be sold just like an object.

### Feudalism

In this system, a person swore personal loyalty to somebody else in exchange for the right to have a certain amount of land for a lifetime.

### Caste

In India, people are traditionally divided into groups according to caste, rather than class. The Hindu religion divides people into categories according to how they are supposed to have behaved in their previous life, because Hindus believe that people have more than one life and are reborn. If you behave badly in one life, you come back as a low caste. If you behave well, you come back as a high caste. The lowest group are the **untouchables**, and the highest caste are the **Brahmin**. You cannot change caste during a lifetime. When a person's position in society is determined by birth, it is known as **ascription**.

Caste is different from social class because:
1 It is based upon the idea that you cannot improve your caste. In British society, it is possible to move up or down the classes, depending partly upon ability.
2 It is derived from religious beliefs; class is not.
3 It does not allow people of different castes to have social relationships or to marry. Class permits this.

### How social class influences our lives

Although most people are not aware of it, our social class strongly influences our lives in many ways. Examples of its influence include:
1 The babies of middle-class people are less likely to die in their first year than the children of the working class (known as lower infant mortality rates).
2 Middle-class people are likely to be healthier throughout their lives than the working class.
3 Middle-class people are likely to live longer than working-class people, on average.
4 Middle-class people have higher incomes.
5 Middle-class people have better housing conditions.
6 Middle-class people are less likely to become unemployed than working-class people.
7 Middle-class people often have different attitudes and values to those of working-class people – for example, they are likely to vote differently, to spend their money on different things and to have different leisure activities.

Figures 1 and 2 illustrate how social class can influence our lives.

### Measuring social class

We know that social class exists, and most people have a vague personal method of dividing people into classes. However, sociologists have some very exact ways of dividing people by class.

### *Occupation and class divisions*
The most commonly used way of dividing people into social class is by their jobs. Sociologists use occupation as the starting point

**Fig. 1** How illness relates to social class. (Class V is the lowest and class I is highest.)

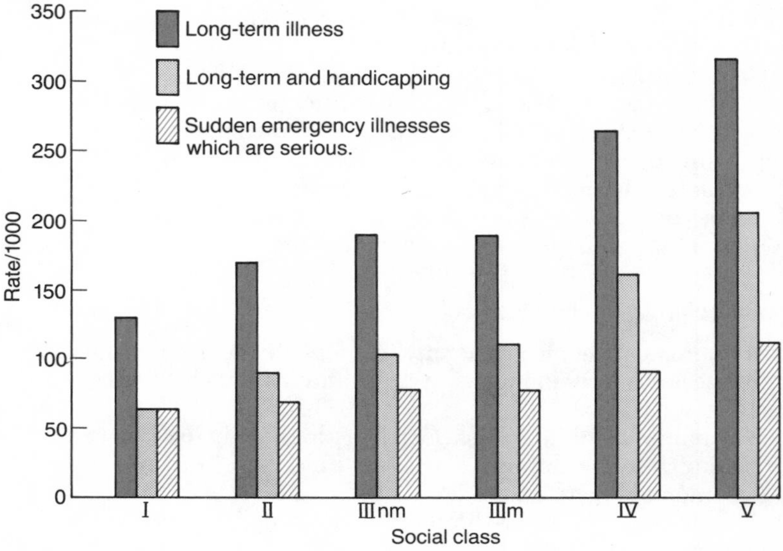

Rates of self-reported illness by social class, per 1000 people –
men and women, all ages, Great Britain.

Source: Blaxter, 1976

for dividing people into social classes because:
1  A person's job decides how much income and prestige they
receive (prestige is how highly people rate a job – compare a
doctor and a milkman, for example).
2  The income earned can influence the lifestyle of a person (what
they spend on leisure activities, and the type of these leisure
activities).
3  A person's job also reflects educational differences.
 There are some problems, however, using occupation to slot
people into different social classes:
1  The same job title can hide very great differences in income.
For example, 'farmer' can mean a man or woman with a very
small farm, struggling to make a living; it can also mean a very
rich person who has thousands of hectares of land.
2  The very rich who do not have to have a job are not included in
this method of measuring social class.

**Fig. 2** Earnings by occupation

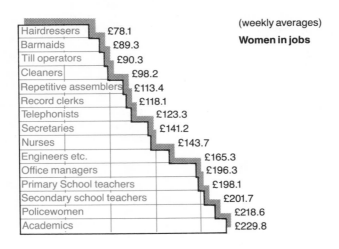

(weekly averages)

**Women in jobs**

|  |  |
| --- | --- |
| Hairdressers | £78.1 |
| Barmaids | £89.3 |
| Till operators | £90.3 |
| Cleaners | £98.2 |
| Repetitive assemblers | £113.4 |
| Record clerks | £118.1 |
| Telephonists | £123.3 |
| Secretaries | £141.2 |
| Nurses | £143.7 |
| Engineers etc. | £165.3 |
| Office managers | £196.3 |
| Primary School teachers | £198.1 |
| Secondary school teachers | £201.7 |
| Policewomen | £218.6 |
| Academics | £229.8 |

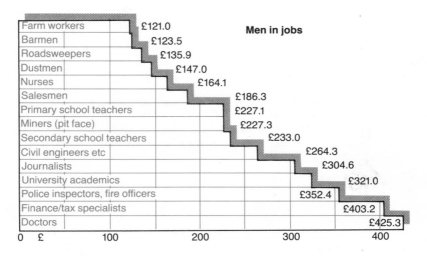

**Men in jobs**

|  |  |
| --- | --- |
| Farm workers | £121.0 |
| Barmen | £123.5 |
| Roadsweepers | £135.9 |
| Dustmen | £147.0 |
| Nurses | £164.1 |
| Salesmen | £186.3 |
| Primary school teachers | £227.1 |
| Miners (pit face) | £227.3 |
| Secondary school teachers | £233.0 |
| Civil engineers etc | £264.3 |
| Journalists | £304.6 |
| University academics | £321.0 |
| Police inspectors, fire officers | £352.4 |
| Finance/tax specialists | £403.2 |
| Doctors | £425.3 |

0    £    100              200              300              400

This table shows the wide variety of salaries paid to people in employment.
The higher the salary the better the standard of living.

Source: *New Society,* 1987

Nevertheless, measures based on occupation are still the simplest and most useful form of placing people within social classes.

The classification of social class used by the Government in official reports is the Registrar General's classification.

**Fig. 3** The Registrar General's classification of social classes

| Social class | Description | Example | Percentage of population |
|---|---|---|---|
| I | Professional executive | Managers Doctors Accountants | 5 |
| II | 'Semi-professionals': managers | Teachers Nurses | 20 |
| III N | Skilled non-manual | Clerical workers | 15 |
| III M | Skilled manual | Taxi drivers Plumbers | 33 |
| IV | Semi-skilled manual | Farmworkers Assembly-line workers | 19 |
| V | Unskilled manual | Building labourers | 8 |

As you can see, occupations are divided into five classes, with class 3 divided into two, between **skilled manual** and **skilled non-manual** jobs (manual means people who work mainly with their hands, often in labouring jobs, while non-manual means people who work in offices and shops).

 The changing class structure

In the 1950s, social class differences were very clear in Britain. The observer could pick out:
1  A working class which was relatively lowly paid, whose members worked in manual jobs, ranging from labourers to skilled workers.
2  A middle class which was better paid and had greater job security. Its members usually worked in non-manual

occupations, ranging from clerical work to lower management.
3  An upper class of the wealthy, who either lived off investments
and had no work, or were owners and directors of large
companies.
Today, however, these class differences have become blurred,
particularly between the middle and the working class.
Differences in such things as income, home ownership, styles of
leisure and ownership of consumer goods have all been narrowed.
It is still true to say that class exists, but it is very different. In
the next three sections we will examine these changes under the
headings, the working class, the middle class and the rich.

## The working class

The traditional working class was employed in manual jobs
earning relatively low wages, and they lived in the inner cities
and in the mining areas. They had very different values from the
middle class, believing very much in the need to 'stick together'
against the bosses. There were, of course, differences between
them – particularly the differences between the skilled and the
unskilled workers.

### Embourgeoisement
In the 1960s, it was suggested that the better-paid sections of the
working class were adopting the lifestyles of the middle class and
that soon virtually all the working class would become part of
the middle class. This process was called **embourgeoisement**.
   Goldthorpe and Lockwood studied a sample of these high-
earning (affluent) workers, to see whether or not they really had
become middle class. They decided that the evidence still
suggested that there were great differences in the values of the
middle-class people and the working-class men (affluent workers)
in their study.

### The 'new' working class
Sociologists do agree, however, that a division has taken place
amongst the working class between those who earn good wages,
are in secure employment, own their own houses and live in the
suburbs, called the **new working class**; and those who are
unemployed or earn low wages, rent their houses and live in
inner-city areas, known as the **traditional working class**.
   These divisions are compounded by the growing differences in
the living standards between the north and south-east of Britain.
The new working class are more likely to be found in the south-
east.

### The middle class

In the last 30 years, the number of people engaged in manual work has declined greatly. Whereas over two thirds of people used to be in manual work, today the figure is a little over one third. Within the middle class, there are two easily identified groups: the white-collar workers and the professionals and managers.

*The white-collar workers*
These are people who do office and shopwork which does not require high qualifications. The amount of this work has increased over the years as technology has changed and more office work has occurred. Increasingly, this sort of work is performed by women. Generally it is fairly low paid, although it has higher status than manual work.

Many sociologists suggest that routine white-collar work should not be considered as middle-class work, but instead be seen as a new type of working-class employment, reflecting the changing technology. The real division lies between the professional/managerial groups and other jobs.

*Professionals and managers*
This group of workers has sometimes been called the **service class**, because they are the ones who are supposed to service the needs of the owners of the factories and offices, by managing and controlling the majority of the workforce.

Professional people are those who are employed (or who work for themselves) in complex work which generally requires high levels of education. They include doctors, accountants and, on the margins, social workers and perhaps teachers. Managers are those who direct the work of others. Professionals are the fastest-growing group in the workforce and have doubled in number in the last 20 years. Managers too have increased in numbers, at a slightly lesser rate.

### The rich

The final class that we need to examine is the rich. This is generally defined as the small group of people who own the vast bulk of wealth and earn the highest incomes

Wealth is usually a form of ownership of companies (stocks and shares) and land. In Britain today, the top 10 per cent own about 55 per cent of all wealth, according to Government statistics. However, many people have suggested that the real amount of wealth held by the top 10 per cent is much higher, because the wealthy underdeclare their wealth in order to avoid tax. These

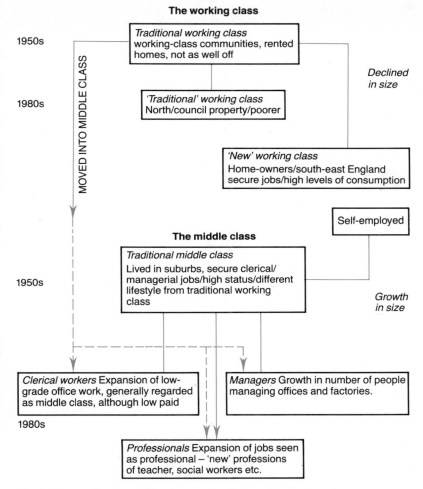

**Fig. 4** The growth of the middle class and the decline of the working class

critics have argued that as much as 72 per cent of the wealth lies in the hands of the top 10 per cent.

Throughout this century there had been a gradual redistribution of wealth from the richest 10 per cent to the better-off half of the population. Since 1980, however, the rich have increased their proportion of society's wealth. This is the result of cuts in taxes for the very rich.

It is commonly believed that it is possible for virtually anyone with enough grit and determination to become rich. Most of the rich, however, have obtained their wealth through **inheritance**, rather than from 'rags to riches'. The situation in the USA is very different, with about 70 per cent of millionaires being self-made men. Incidentally, the word **men** is important here, as there are very few self-made women and generally wealth is passed down from father to son. It would appear that women from wealthy backgrounds marry into similarly rich backgrounds.

The rich in this country can be divided into three very broad groups:

1  The traditional upper class, who own large amounts of land.
2  The owners of industry and commerce. Although most of these came from rich backgrounds, some of them are people who are self-made.
3  The smaller group of people who have made their wealth through good fortune, such as the most successful entertainers. It is important to realize that wealth and power are closely linked. The owners of large corporations are able to present their views to the Government directly, or through close contact with top civil servants. Many studies have shown that the wealthy and those who occupy the most important positions in Government – Cabinet Ministers, top civil servants and judges – are very often drawn from the public schools. The newspapers too are dominated by a few powerful, rich men who are able to have their views presented regularly through their papers.

### Two explanations for social-class divisions

There are a number of explanations for the existence of social class. Two important ones are those of Karl Marx who lived in the last century, was a communist and the founder of the political and social movement called **Marxism**, and Max Weber, who was writing at the turn of this century and who has had a very great influence on the development of Sociology.

**K**  *The Marxist explanation for social class*
Writing in the last century, Karl Marx pointed out that there was really only one division that was important in society – that of ownership of property. Most people then, and to a lesser exent now, own very little in the way of property. Most of us get our living by working for other people. In Marxist terms, we sell our labour. Marx called everybody who has to work in order to earn a living, the **proletariat**, or the working class.

On the other hand, there are those who own the companies people work for. Some of these people may work, but generally need not. Those who own the factories and commercial institutions are called the **bourgeoisie**, or the ruling class.

For Marx, then, there are two classes: the owners (the bourgeoisie) and the workers (the proletariat). The proletariat work for the bourgeoisie. Marx predicted that the numbers of the owners would decline and they would become very rich. On the other hand, the numbers of the workers would increase and they would become poor. Eventually, the workers would rebel in anger and desperation.

Marx's theory can be criticized because the idea that the numbers of the rich would decrease and that the workers would get poorer has proved false. Since the 1950s in Britain, the workers have had a rising standard of living. The simple division into owners and workers ignores the huge growth in jobs which are well paid and have high status, such as the professions and the managers. These people are not owners, but do have a similar standard of living.

### Weber's explanation for social class

Max Weber wrote at the beginning of this century that social class was based upon three things: differences in income and wealth, differences in the status that people held, and differences in the amount of power they had to get people to do things in their interest. Weber said that people varied in how much of each of these they had, and that just because someone was wealthy, it did not mean that they had high status or great power. For example, today, priests may not have wealth or power, but they have high status in most people's eyes; on the other hand, successful used-car salesmen may earn a lot of money, and yet have little status.

### Social mobility

Social mobility is the movement of people up and down the social classes. For instance, **upward social mobility** would be the move from being a clerk in an office to being a manager. There are various types of social mobility.

1 **Intergenerational mobility**, the social class position of a person compared to their father's position.

2 **Intragenerational mobility**, the social class position of a person now compared to the social class level of their first job.

3 **Short-range mobility**, when a person only moves slightly up or down the class structure.

4 **Long-range mobility**, when a person moves a lot, up or down the class structure.

Social mobility is important because it tells us just how 'open'

British society is. By this, we mean that the greater the movement of people up or down, the more likely it is that people get their jobs on their abilities, rather than through their parents.

The pattern of intergenerational mobility since the 1950s indicates that there is a general upward movement. Far more people are entering the professions and the managerial jobs than ever before from the classes lower down. Fewer people are moving down, however. This is partly because there has been a large growth in the number of professional and managerial level jobs available, so there has been plenty of room for those drawn from the working and lower middle class.

The pattern of intragenerational mobility is rather different. It suggests that, increasingly, people are likely to enter employment at certain levels and to remain within those levels. It was once easier for people to work their way up in a company, starting from the bottom, than it is now. This can partly be explained by the fact that education now plays a very important part in job prospects. Companies recruit people direct into management, for example, from universities – rarely do they promote people from clerical backgrounds into managerial posts. So, children with working-class parents who do well in education can go straight into top jobs, while those who enter companies at humble levels are less likely to be able successfully to work their way up.

K ▶ *Reasons for social mobility*
Explanations for the amount of social mobility that people have include the following:

**1 Changing occupational structure** The greater the number of higher level jobs available, the greater the chance of those from working-class backgrounds moving into these jobs. In the last 20 years there has been a great increase in the number of professional and managerial jobs available.

**2 The birth rate of the higher classes** The fewer children the people from the managerial and professional backgrounds have, the less chance they have of taking all the top positions, so the chances of the working class increase.

**3 Education** The greater the educational level of a person, the greater their chance of getting a high-level job.

**4 Individual's attitudes** Certain people have a far greater determination to succeed than others. This could well be the result of upbringing. It has been suggested that middle-class parents are far more likely to stress the importance of career and education than some working-class parents.

**5 Sex** Women are less likely to move upward through employment than men. This is generally because women are expected to treat their career as less important than their children (unlike the husbands). Child-raising often prevents women from gaining promotion, as it takes women out of the workforce in their late twenties/early thirties, just when the highest chances of promotion occur.

**6 Race** There appears to be obstacles in the way of many of those from the ethnic minorities, which prevent them gaining employment and promotion.

**7 Area** Increasingly the differences in the numbers of jobs available in the north and the south-east have meant that it is easier to get on in the south. In the north, there are far fewer top jobs.

## Wealth, income and power

In Britain there are great differences in the amount of wealth, income and power that people have. On the one hand there are relatively few people who are extremely rich and able to wield considerable power. On the other hand there is the majority of the population, who live off their wage, have little wealth, apart from their own homes, and have little influence on the political decisions made.

### Wealth

Wealth means assets which are worth money when sold. It usually consists of shares and property. There is considerable disagreement over how to measure wealth, and this influences the statistics concerning wealth distribution. However, one study conducted for London Weekend Television in 1986 concluded that the richest 1 per cent of the population own 21 per cent of the wealth in Britain, and the top 5 per cent own 41 per cent of the wealth.

**Fig. 5** Distribution of wealth

| % of the population | No of people | Total share of wealth |
|---|---|---|
| 0.1 | 43 500 | 7 |
| 1 | 435 000 | 21 |
| 5 | 2 175 000 | 41 |
| Bottom 50 | 21 750 000 | 4 |

**Fig. 6** Snakes and ladders game

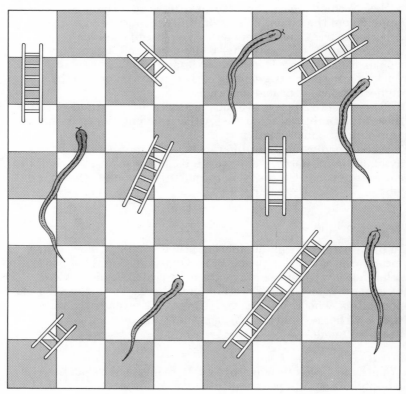

Wealth, income, and opportunities are determined by many factors, some of which are listed below:

| *'Snakes'* | *'Ladders'* |
|---|---|
| racial prejudice | education |
| unemployment | determination to succeed |
| sexual discrimination | mobility |
| large families | inherited wealth |
| illness | family planning |
| injury | more professional jobs |
| disability | vocational training |
| old age | welfare benefits |

The most common method of becoming rich is quite simply to have parents who are rich. In Britain about two-thirds of millionaires came from wealthy backgrounds (though their parents were not necessarily millionaires). However, a fifth of millionaires come from humble origins.

People obtain their wealth through land, the stock market, and service industries; less often through industry.

*Income*

Income is the money that a person receives through employment, investment or from the State (as social security, for example). Income is unevenly distributed, like wealth, but the gap between the highest and lowest incomes is not so great. The top 1 per cent of earners have 5 per cent of pre-tax income; the top 10 per cent have 25 per cent of pre-tax income. Taxation does not appear to have much effect in taking money from the wealthy and passing it to the less well off.

The proportion of wealth owned by the richest 5 per cent has declined considerably this century. However, this has not moved to the poorest sections of the population, but to the richest 20 per cent. There has been a redistribution of wealth *within* the rich.

**Fig. 7** How the distribution of wealth has changed 1911-86

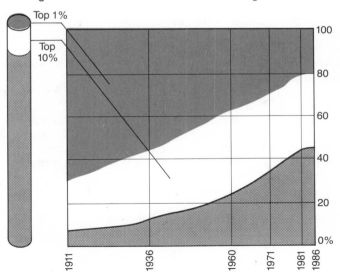

Source : *New Society,* 1986

*Power*
There is a close relationship between wealth and power. Those who own large amounts of wealth in Britain are usually able to influence political decisions in a number of ways:
1 The ownership of the newspapers is in the hands of very few individuals, who have the power to influence public opinion.
2 The wealthy are often closely connected to each other and those in politics, through marriage ties and attendance at the same schools.
3 Those who own offices and factories can always influence Government thinking, by threatening to take their factories or investments to another country.

## Summary

1 Social class is not the only form of stratification. In Britain today, there are also important divisions by sex, ethnic group and age. In history, there has been feudalism, castes and slavery.
2 Social class influences our lives in a number of important ways, ranging from health to leisure.
3 Sociologists usually measure social class by occupation.
4 The divisions between the middle and working classes have grown smaller.
5 The working class has become divided between the new working class and the traditional working class. An important element of this is the north/south divide.
6 In the middle class, the divisions lie between white-collar workers and managers/professionals.
7 There are different explanations for social class. Two of these are Weber's and Marx's.
8 Social mobility is movement up or down the social classes.
9 There have been quite high rates of social mobility since 1945, mainly because of the changing occupational structure.
10 There has been some redistribution of wealth in Britain over the last 50 years.
11 A small proportion of the population owns the bulk of the wealth.
12 Wealth, income and power are all linked.

## Revision questions

1 Give three examples of the importance of social class in our lives.

**2** Why do sociologists use occupation as a way of measuring social class?

**3** What is meant by the term, the 'new working class'? Can you suggest reasons why this is an important change in the working class?

**4** What differences are there between routine white-collar workers and professionals/managers?

**5** What two classes are there in the Marxist model of social class? What are the differences in the social classes based upon?

**6** What influences the extent of a person's social mobility?

**7** Explain the relationship between income, wealth and power.

**8** Look at fig. 1.
(a) Which social class has the worst health?
(b) Overall, what comment can you make on the relationship between social class and health?

**9** Look at fig. 3. What proportion of the population is in social class II?

**10** Look at fig. 7. What proportion of wealth do the top 1 per cent own?

# 6 Race

## Aims of the chapter

In this chapter we will examine:

**1** The distinction between racial groups and ethnic groups.

**2** The patterns of immigration and the reasons for this.

**3** Where the ethnic minorities settled in Britain, and the reasons for these settlement patterns.

**4** The meaning of racism and discrimination.

**5** Explanations for racist attitudes.

**6** The different life chances experienced by the ethnic minorities.

**Racial groups** is the term that is used to define a group who are presumed to have some special biological features that mark them off from other groups. There are no such things as 'pure' races. Over the millions of years of mankind's history the 'races' have overlapped and intermingled.

**Ethnic groups** is a term used to distinguish groups which have a common culture. The term **ethnic minority** is used to distinguish a group sharing a common culture who are a minority in a society with a different culture. The ethnic minority are usually immigrants or the descendants of immigrants.

## Patterns of immigration

Up to 1962 it was not particularly difficult for immigrants to enter Britain. From 1962 onwards, however, a series of laws has been passed to restrict the numbers of non European Community persons allowed into Britain. Very few immigrants are allowed into Britain today.

Historically, Britain has had a number of 'waves' of immigrants. The largest number was probably the Irish immigrants who came in the second half of the last century, followed by Jews escaping from Central and Eastern Europe.

Between 1950 and 1961 a large number of people from the West Indies and the Asian subcontinent (Indians and Pakistanis) arrived, and a smaller number of Chinese. In total, however, the immigrants formed less than 1 per cent of the population.

After the 1962 Act, the numbers of immigrants dropped considerably, especially those from the West Indies. The majority of immigrants from the Asian subcontinent were relatives rejoining their family already here. The interest in the levels of immigration and the passing of laws restricting the numbers of immigrants was based largely on the fact that the immigrants were mainly black.

## Reasons for immigration

These can be divided into two – **push** reasons and **pull** reasons.

*Push reasons*
**1 Poverty and unemployment in the country of origin** The immigrants were fleeing dreadful poverty. This poverty had persisted despite British colonial rule.
**2 Persecution** Some groups, East African Asians for instance, were expelled from the African countries they were born in, as an act of deliberate persecution by the local governments. The Asians were British passport-holders.

*Pull reasons*
**1 Labour shortage in Britain** Throughout the 1950s Britain encouraged immigration from the Commonwealth, as there was a shortage of workers for the jobs available. Right through the 1960s and 1970s recruitment continued for people with high

qualifications, such as doctors.

**2 To join relatives** Seventy per cent of immigrants arriving in the 1980s were dependent relatives of people already here.

## Settlement patterns

The immigrants went to the areas where there were jobs:
1 Parts of Yorkshire and Lancashire, to work in the textile industry, which was desperate for cheap labour.
2 The West Midlands for labouring jobs, or Birmingham itself for the service industries.
3 The prosperous south-east, where there was a labour shortage for all sorts of lower-paid work.

Within these areas they settled in the poorest inner-city areas. The reasons for this were:
1 Discrimination – people would neither sell nor rent houses to them in the better areas.
2 The fact that they could not afford to pay for better quality housing outside these areas.
3 Later, as the original immigrants settled in these areas, forming a community, new arrivals were attracted by this and settled too.

The result of these patterns of settlement is that the children of the original immigrants were brought up in these areas, and so the ethnic minority communities increased considerably in number.

## Racism and discrimination

**Racial prejudice** is when people are disliked solely on grounds of ethnic origin or skin colour. This is closely linked with **racism**: the idea that there are very clear racial groupings, each having particular characteristics and behaviour. **Racial discrimination** (or **racialism**) is when people are treated differently solely on the basis of ethnic origin or skin colour. **Institutional racism** is when Blacks and Asians suffer as a result of discrimination against them which is built-in to society and is not deliberate on any individual person's part. For example, it has been shown that many school teachers assume that children of West Indian origin are less likely to be academically successful at school. This affects the way they act towards them. However, the teachers are not necessarily prejudiced.

## Explanations for racism and discrimination

Explanations include:
**1 The authoritarian personality** Certain people are brought

up with very rigid ideas about the world, and this includes intolerance of others who are different.

**2 Stereotyping** In the past, Britain controlled many other territories, which were its colonies. In order, perhaps, to justify this, beliefs developed which stressed that Blacks and Asians, in particular, were inferior and were not 'civilized'. These attitudes have lingered on in stereotypes.

**3 Scapegoating** It is often difficult to understand the true reasons for periods of economic crisis and high unemployment. It is much easier to blame less powerful groups, who provide clear scapegoats for the problems. If they can be made to go away (or murdered, as in Nazi Germany) then the problems will also go away. In Britain, Blacks and Asians have often been used as the scapegoats for unemployment, inner-city problems and the high crime rates. This is encouraged by the media and by some politicians.

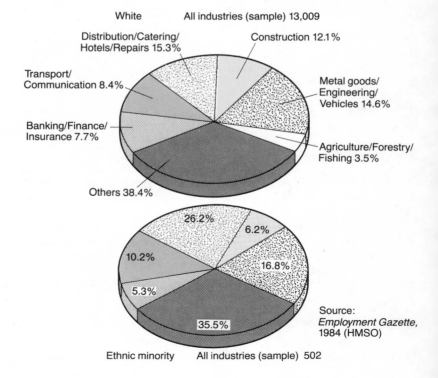

**Fig. 1** The industries ethnic minorities work in (*% employed or on government schemes*)

White     All industries (sample) 13,009

Distribution/Catering/Hotels/Repairs 15.3%

Construction 12.1%

Transport/Communication 8.4%

Metal goods/Engineering/Vehicles 14.6%

Banking/Finance/Insurance 7.7%

Agriculture/Forestry/Fishing 3.5%

Others 38.4%

26.2%   6.2%

10.2%

16.8%

5.3%

35.5%

Source: *Employment Gazette*, 1984 (HMSO)

Ethnic minority     All industries (sample) 502

► Life chances and ethnic group

*Employment*
Those of West Indian origin are likely to be over-represented in skilled manual work, and strongly under-represented in white-collar and managerial jobs. Those of Asian descent are less likely than Whites to be in managerial, professional and white-collar occupations, but there are greater proportions of them in these jobs than those of West Indian origin. Those of Asian origin have high rates of self-employment and small business ownership.
1 **Wages** Blacks and Asians are overwhelmingly in the lower-paid groups in British society.
2 **Hours of work** A 1985 survey showed that Blacks were more likely to work shift hours than Whites.
3 **Promotion** The 1985 survey showed that rates of promotion were much lower for Blacks and Asians than for Whites.

*Unemployment*

**Fig. 2**  Unemployment and the ethnic minorities

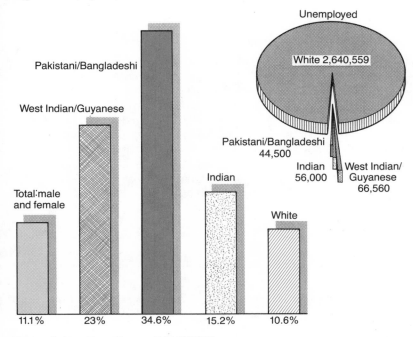

Source: *Labour Force Survey,* 1984 (HMSO)

Unemployment rates for Blacks and Asians are significantly higher than they are for Whites. Those of West Indian origin have twice the national average unemployment rate. Those of Pakistani/Bangladeshi origin have almost three times the national unemployment rate.

*Housing*

Housing conditions are different for the members of the ethnic minorities than for the majority of the population. Those of West Indian origin are likely to be over-represented in council housing. The council property they have is likely to be older and of poorer quality than average. Those of Asian origin have higher than average rates of home-ownership. However, the properties they own are likely to be in poor condition and to lack certain amenities.

*Education*

Blacks are overall amongst the worst performers in the education system. Those of Indian origin, however, perform well.

*Politics*

Blacks and Asians are barely represented in Parliament.

### Getting rid of racism in Britain

Laws have been passed to eliminate racial discrimination. In particular, the 1965 Race Relations Act made it illegal to discriminate, and there is a Commission for Racial Equality which enforces the law and promotes the cause of racial equality.

Attitudes are more difficult to change. A *New Society* survey of young people's attitudes found a majority consider themselves to be prejudiced. The best way to combat racist attitudes seems to be by adjusting the way people are taught at school. There are now race advisers in some education authorities, advising teachers on the best methods to teach which will help to eliminate racist attitudes.

## Summary

1 There are no such things as clearly definable 'racial groups'. Instead, there are 'ethnic groups', which consist of people with common origins and cultures.
2 In Britain the main ethnic minorities from the West Indies and

Asia arrived in the 1950s and 1960s because there were many job opportunities available here.

**3** Most ethnic groups settled in the areas of the country where there were jobs. These were parts of Yorkshire and Lancashire, the Midlands and the south-east.

**4** They settled in the run-down inner-city areas. This was mainly because they were unable to obtain accommodation anywhere else.

**5** Many Whites are racist.

**6** Explanations for this include authoritarian personality, stereotyping and scapegoating.

**7** The life chances of Blacks and Asians in Britain are often worse than those of Whites.

**8** Blacks and Asians are more likely to be found in worse jobs, to be unemployed, and to live in poorer quality housing. Many of them do not fulfil their potential in the education system.

**9** Attempts have been made to eliminate racial discrimination, but they have not been completely successful, as people still have racist views.

## Revision questions

**1** What are the differences between an 'ethnic minority' and a 'race'?

**2** Suggest any three reasons why people came to live in Britain.

**3** Explain why the ethnic minorities are concentrated in certain parts of the big towns and cities.

**4** What is 'institutional racism'?

**5** Explain the meaning of the term 'scapegoating'.

**6** Give examples of three areas where the life chances of Blacks and Asians are significantly worse than those of Whites.

**7** Look at fig. 2. What are the unemployment rates for:

(a) Pakistanis/Bangladeshis?

(b) West Indians?

(c) Which group has the lowest unemployment rate?

# 7 Gender

## Aims of the chapter

In this chapter we will examine:

1 The distinction between sex and gender.
2 The importance of gender roles.
3 How gender roles are learned.
4 The situation of women in employment.
5 The situation of women involved in domestic labour.
6 The changing status of women in society.

### Sex and gender

There is an important distinction between sex and gender.
**Sex** refers to the biological differences between men and women.
**Gender** refers to the socially constructed roles which men and
women have. Gender is social, not biological.

### Gender roles

As soon as we are born we learn that only some forms of
behaviour are appropriate for people in the same gender as
ourselves. We are encouraged and rewarded for conforming to
these **gender roles**. Girls are supposed to be more emotional,
physically weaker, less outward going and less aggressive than
boys.

 If these roles were natural, then we would expect them to be the
same in every society. This is not true, however. In many
societies, such as the USSR, the women do as much physical work
as the men. In at least one African society, the Ik, studied by
Colin Turnbull, the motherly instinct is completely missing. In
other societies, it is the men who dress up and enjoy dancing, not
the women. In fact every stereotype we have about men and
women can be contradicted by their behaviour in some societies.

 In summary, gender roles are learned, they are not the outcome
of natural, biological differences.

 ### Socialization into gender roles

Gender socialization is performed by the family, the school, the
media and the wider culture of society.

*The family*
1 Parents expect different behaviour from boys and girls. They
may expect boys to be rough and aggressive. Girls are expected to
be quieter and more gentle. If the girl behaves differently then

she is labelled a 'tomboy'. The boy may be called a 'cissy' if he is not rough.

**2** The toys are different: boys are more likely to get construction, sporting and war-based toys. Girls are given dolls, prams, cookers, and so on.

**3** The language used is different: girls are described as 'pretty' and 'sweet', while boys are described as 'rascals' or 'little horrors' (in an affectionate way!)

**4** The clothes they wear are different: girls in dresses, often having long hair and the boys with jeans and tracksuits, with shorter hair.

*The school*

**1** Male and female pupils are treated differently by teachers, who have different expectations of them.

**2** They are encouraged to follow different courses of study – for girls it is secretarial, domestic and social sciences and the humanities. For boys it is the sciences and technology.

**3** Boys are more likely to get teacher attention.

**4** The way that girls and boys learn appropriate behaviour is known as the **hidden curriculum**.

*The media*

The media, particularly the mass-market 'tabloid' newspapers, give two images of women – those of either being a 'caring' person or being a 'sexy' person. Pin-ups, and the descriptions of women ('busty, blonde, 23-year-old'), reinforce the importance of looks to women.

On the other hand, there is also a stress on the caring and mothering aspects of the female role. Women are given recipes, knitting patterns and advice on how to be a good wife. Advertising strengthens these two distinct images of women, in its portrayal of women in advertisements on television and in newspapers/magazines.

*The wider culture of society*

This pulls all this together and constantly imposes constraints on people who wish to break out of their gender roles. The **peer group** is particularly important here, especially to young people. Anyone failing to conform to the peer group's accepted behaviour, for instance an 'effeminate' man, would be laughed at and made the subject of jokes, or derided in some other way.

The significance of gender in women's lives

**In childhood** Girls are expected to stay in more, to help their mothers with housework, and parents are likely to maintain stricter control over them.

**In eduation**  Girls are more likely to choose arts and domestic-science courses. Girls do at least as well as boys at school, but are more likely to drop out of the education system at an earlier age.

**In employment**  Women are more often in low-paid jobs. Almost half are in part-time employment and they have restricted opportunities of promotion.

**In the home**  Women are expected to do most of the housework and be responsible for the children.

**In social life**  Women's lives are constrained by the fact they are female. There are certain places they cannot go by themselves (e.g. pubs) and many things that they cannot do (e.g. walking home alone late at night) and certain ways they are not expected to behave (e.g. swearing) simply because they are women.

### Women and work

Throughout this century the number of women in paid employment has increased. Today, almost half the workforce is comprised of women, and the proportion is still increasing. The increase in the number of women working is mainly a result of married women going out to work.

The reasons for the increase in the numbers of women working are:

1  The changing nature of the economy – there has been a shift away from heavy industry (steel and engineering) to light industry (electronics) and services (banking, insurance) in which more women are likely to be employed.

2  Women are often treated as a cheap source of labour for employers. On average, women earn about 70 per cent of male rates.

3  Women are more willing to work part-time, and so are far more flexible than full-time employees – 90 per cent of all part-time workers are female.

4  Women want to work, rather than be housewives.

5  Women now have fewer children, within a shorter period. This means that there are more women available for work.

The effects on the family life of women working are:

1  Women no longer have to rely on their husbands for income.

2  This independence gives them greater equality in the family.

3  Increasingly, when men are laid off, their wives become the main income earner of the family – this has consequences for the traditional husband/wife roles. It may be the man who looks after

the children, cooks and cleans.
4  There is evidence to suggest that many men find it difficult to accept this change in roles. This may lead to conflict.

*The types of work that women do*
Two thirds of women are concentrated in just three types of work:
1  **Clerical work** This is routine office and secretarial work.
2  **Service work** This covers a range of occupations, from shop assistant to bank employee.
3  **Professional and technical services** This may sound impressive, but it often involves working in the lowest-paid areas of the professions – such as nursing (92 per cent of nurses are female).

Overall, women are employed in a narrow range of occupations, which are low paid.

**Fig. 1**  Where women work

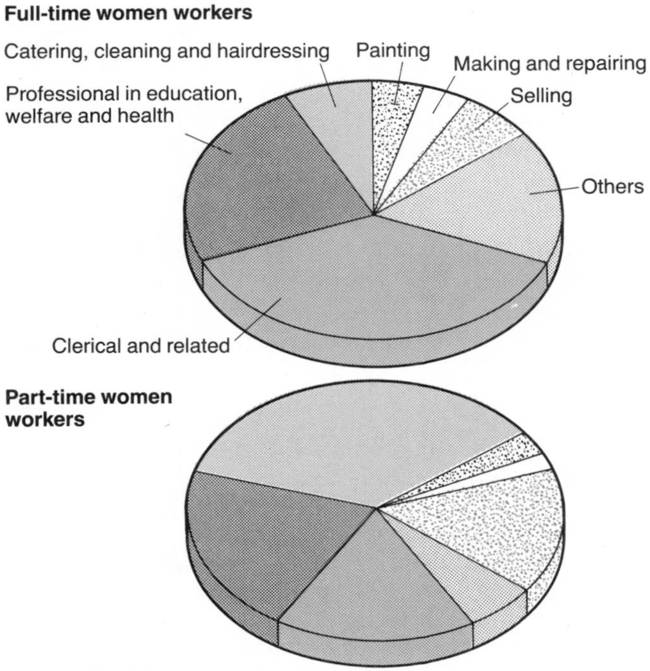

**Full-time women workers**

Catering, cleaning and hairdressing     Painting     Making and repairing

Professional in education, welfare and health     Selling

Others

Clerical and related

**Part-time women workers**

(Great Britain, 1985)

Source: *Department of Employment*, 1985 (HMSO)

▶ *Promotion and level of work*
In 1985, only about 10 per cent of all women were in the higher grades of professional and managerial work, compared to 23 per cent of all male employees. Only 13 per cent of 'skilled' workers are female. There is only a small percentage of female doctors, dentists, solicitors and accountants, for example. Women are less often promoted than men because:
1 They often have to interrupt their careers at a crucial time (late 20s) to have children and spend a few years looking after them. They then return to work, but have often been overtaken by their male colleagues who have not had a break in their working lives.
2 The employers and managers are usually male and may be suspicious that women will not return after having children (though this is increasingly rare) and so do not promote them to senior posts.

▶ *Wages*
Sixty per cent of women are found in the 10 lowest-paid occupations. Women earn, on average, about 70 per cent of male wages. This continues even though the Equal Pay Act states that men and women must be paid the same for similar types of work.
   The differences in earning occur because women are concentrated in low-paid, low-status work with little chance of doing overtime.

▶ *Hours of work*
Almost half of female employees are in part-time employment. The reasons are that many employers prefer to employ part-time workers to full-time workers, because they are flexible and cheap, and women look for part-time work because it fits in with their family commitments.

▶ *Housework*
Work is usually taken to mean paid employment outside the home. Housework too is work, but is has certain special characteristics:
1 **It is unpaid** Housewives receive no salary.
2 **It is low-status work** Indeed it is not even considered as work.
3 **It is boring** One study, by Oakley, found that it was as boring as assembly line work.
4 **It is lonely** Housewives are generally cut off, with no contact except for young children.
5 **Long hours** On average housewives worked 77 hours per week, in Oakley's study.

**Fig. 2** How women are concentrated in low-paid employment

The low paid (earnings 1986)

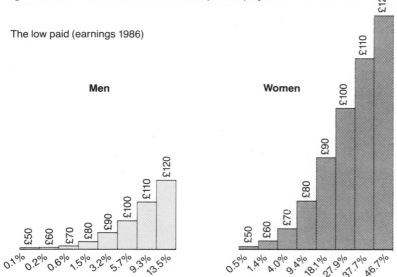

The percentage of men and women earning less than £120 (in 1986)

Source: *New Society*, 1987

**Fig. 3** The growth of part-time work

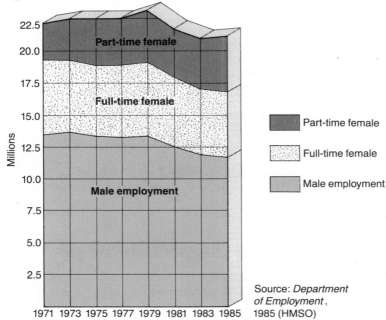

Source: *Department of Employment*, 1985 (HMSO)

**6** It is almost **exclusively female** work. There are few male 'househusbands' (though this may increase as male unemployment continues to increase).

### The changing status of women

Men and women have equal legal and political rights today. It is now illegal to discriminate against a person on the grounds of sex, and there is a Government funded organization, **The Equal Opportunities Commission**, to ensure that women have equal chances to men. There is also a law which states that men and women must be paid the same for equivalent work. This has been the outcome of a long struggle.

About 100 years ago, women had very few rights and were commonly regarded as inferior to men:
**1** This was the result of the fact that women had been edged out of paid employment by men, except for domestic service employment. This lack of jobs meant that they lost their economic independence.
**2** Women had no property rights (property was always in the name of the husband).
**3** They could not obtain divorces (except if violence was used against them by their husbands).
**4** They had little chance of education.
**5** Most of their adult lives were taken up with childbearing.
The reasons for the rise in the position of women:
**1** The increasing job opportunities have meant that they can obtain work and become financially independent of husbands and fathers.
**2** There have been improvements in educational opportunities for women.
**3** The decrease in the number of children has released women from a life of childbearing.
**4** Legal changes: as a result of pressure group activity by women, they have managed to have the laws altered to give them equal opportunities.

*The situation today*
Although women are politically and legally equal to men, it is important to remember that they still face a number of problems which prevent total equality with men.
**1** They earn less on average than men (because of the sorts of job they do).
**2** They are still prevented from doing certain things, because of

social taboos – this restricts their behaviour in sexual and social areas.

**3** They are still expected to perform the bulk of domestic work in the home.

**4** They are still heavily under-represented in the top positions in society – in managerial jobs, in ownership of companies, in politics.

## Summary

**1** 'Sex' refers to biological distinctions. 'Gender' refers to socially created distinctions between the sexes.

**2** People learn gender roles in childhood through a process of socialization.

**3** The main agencies of socialization are the family, the school and the media.

**4** Women have significantly different experiences of life than men, in areas such as education, work, family life, etc.

**5** Women are concentrated in low-paid occupations with less chances of promotion than men.

**6** In the home, it is usually women who are expected to perform the bulk of the housework and to care for the children.

**7** A hundred years ago, women had very low status in society and few legal rights. As a result of the struggle by women for equal rights, their status has improved greatly.

**8** Today they are legally equal to men, although in practice they still have worse life chances than many men.

## Revision questions

**1** Explain the meaning of gender roles.

**2** Explain how females are socialized into gender roles by the family.

**3** Give two examples of how gender is important in influencing the lives of women.

**4** Give three reasons for the increase in women working.

**5** What effects might the employment of women have on family life?

**6** Why are women less likely to be promoted than men?

**7** If women are legally entitled to equal pay, how is it possible for women to earn only 70 per cent of average male wages?

**8** Give two reasons for the rise in the status of women.

**9** Look at fig. 1. What is the most common type of employment for women, in full-time employment?
**10** Look at fig. 2.
(a) Who earns less money on average – men or women?
(b) What percentage of women workers earned less than £100 per week in 1986?

## 8 Education

## Aims of the chapter

In this chapter we will examine:

**1** The distinctions between formal and informal education.
**2** The importance of the hidden curriculum.
**3** How the peer group can influence educational success/failure.
**4** The changes in the education system and the reasons for these changes.
**5** The reasons why some working-class children fail to fulfil their full potential, which include such things as the home environment, the neighbourhood, the role of teachers and the school itself.
**6** The differences in the educational experiences of males and females.
**7** The poor performances of some of the ethnic minorities in the educational system.

### Socialization and education

There is a clear distinction between **formal** and **informal** learning.

*Formal learning*
This is the type of academic or practical learning that people are taught in schools and colleges. It consists of clearly defined skills taught in lessons in such a way that they can be graded through examinations, for example, Maths. Formal learning is the type of learning that is **supposed** to take place at school.

*Informal learning*
This form of learning is part of the general socialization process, through which we learn to be normal members of society. Informal learning is not organized or examined, and it is learnt through casual, daily contact with other people around us. The most important people are the family and the peer group (people of our own age), and also teachers.

In modern, complex societies such as our own, much of the learning process takes place in schools through formal learning. In most societies throughout history learning has been informal, through casual contact, each generation passing on its knowledge to the next.

Even in schools, much of what we learn is through informal learning. Although teachers may officially be teaching a particular subject, for example, English Language, in fact they may also be teaching attitudes and skills which are no part of English. In order to teach a certain point, the teacher may get the pupils to read something on life in a factory. The pupils are not just learning English, they are also learning about work and developing attitudes to it.

*The hidden curriculum*
This unofficial learning is known as the 'hidden curriculum' and is learnt from teachers and also from the peer group. It is called the hidden curriculum because the correct term for the subjects we learn at school is the 'curriculum', and the informal learning is hidden within this. Gradually expectations and ideas are learned through contact with others at school.

Examples of the hidden curriculum are:
1 **Gender roles** Teachers act differently towards boys and girls (although they may not realize this) and help to develop different attitudes and patterns of behaviour between them.
2 **Racial attitudes** Like gender differences, pupils become aware of differences in ethnic groups, through the attitudes of teachers and other pupils, and the content of textbooks.
3 **Social class differences** The importance of social class and its relationship to such things as income, the way people speak, differences in housing and possibly clothing can all be found at school. There is some evidence that teachers prefer middle-class children and are more sympathetic to them.
4 **Social control and preparation for work** Apart from actual subjects taught at school, pupils also learn to be obedient and they are encouraged to work hard. This prepares them for work later in life.

*The peer group*

People with whom we identify and whose behaviour we copy are
known as the peer group. At school, this is usually the other
pupils with whom we are friendly (or whom we admire). The peer
group is extremely important in understanding pupils'
behaviour. In lower streams, the pupils will be more likely to
'muck around' and pupils who are attentive and hard working
will be the object of jokes and will be outsiders. This places
pressure on pupils not to work hard. The opposite is true in the
higher streams.

One study, by Willis, showed that by 'mucking about' at school,
the pupils in lower streams coped with what they saw as
irrelevant and boring; they also ensured their own failure.
However, the very mucking about was just the skill they needed
to cope with the boring jobs that they would eventually get. In
short, the pupils prepared themselves to cope with boring jobs,
without realizing it.

## Educational change

Education for everyone started in 1870, because the Government
was worried that there were not enough people who could read
and write. Without these abilities, it was believed that Britain
would fall behind other industrial nations.

Until 1944, the educational system in Britain developed along
the lines that everyone got a basic education, but only those who
could afford it carried on beyond the age of 13 or 14. Education
was therefore divided along class and gender lines. Only the
middle and upper classes could afford to send their children to
grammar schools, and it was often considered not worth the
money to pay for a girl's education.

In 1944, the Butler Education Act was passed, which said that
all children should be given a test to assess what abilities they
had, and should then be sent to a school which was most
appropriate for them. The examination was the 11+, and there
were three types of school: grammars for the most able, secondary
moderns for the less able, and secondary technicals for the
technically minded (very few built). The system was known as the
tripartite system. The idea behind this was that education should
be based upon ability not on payment. This is known as
meritocracy. Public schools for the rich continued alongside these
schools.

By the 1960s there were many criticisms of this type of school
system. The main one was that too few intelligent working-class

children were getting into grammar schools. The Government introduced comprehensive schools, which took everybody from a certain neighbourhood. By 1986 about 90 per cent of secondary pupils attended comprehensives.

Comprehensives are criticized because:
1 They slow down the cleverest children.
2 The huge schools are large and impersonal.
3 They are not really of mixed social class, because they are based on neighbourhoods. In Britain neighbourhoods are usually dominated by one social class. So inner-city comprehensives are working class and suburban ones are generally middle class.

Comprehensives are defended because:
1 They help to break down class barriers by mixing all children together.
2 They give the working class greater chances than they would have had otherwise.
3 They provide a wide variety of facilities.

## Summary of arguments

1 There is no reliable evidence to support the view that comprehensives slow down the most able.
2 They have improved the exam results of the middle-ability pupils.
3 They do not mix the social classes.

### Recent changes in the education system
In the 1980s the education system has been changed once again. The emphasis for the majority of pupils is increasingly on learning **skills** rather than knowledge. This has resulted in new types of examinations and courses, for example TVEI, GCSE, CPVE, etc. There is more training for work (vocational) after finishing school, such as YTS, and there are plans to introduce new types of school called city technical colleges which will specialize in technology and science. Children of high ability can apply to go to certain public schools, under the assisted places scheme.

### Social class and educational achievement
Certain groups in society appear to perform particularly badly in our education system. One of these groups is the working class (see fig. 1 overleaf).

Explanations include:
1 **Lower intelligence** It has been suggested that the working

**Fig. 1** Class and educational success

Students in higher education by father's occupational group

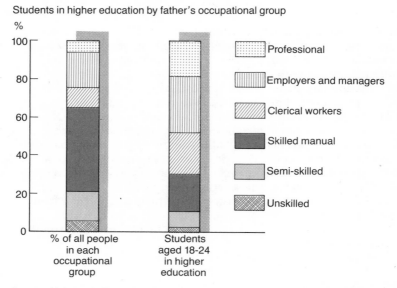

Source: (Adapted) *Social Trends,* 1984 (HMSO)

class are less intelligent. This has been hotly disputed, as there is disagreement over the meaning and measurement of intelligence.

**2   The importance of the home** Parents' interests and encouragement in education seem to be a crucial influence on success at school. It appears that middle-class parents are more likely to give help than are working class parents. The form of language used in the home is important. Bernstein suggested that there are two codes of speech we all use – **elaborated** and **restricted**. Elaborated speech is used in formal situations and is the sort of language which is required in school. Restricted speech is the sort of informal speech we use with friends. He claimed that it was more likely that middle-class parents would use elaborated speech in the home and so their children would become better at its use. The physical condition of the home can affect a child's chances of success. Poor families in damp, overcrowded homes, who have inadequate diets, are at a disadvantage.

**3   The neighbourhood** The local environment in which we are brought up can influence us in many ways. The area may be poor, with worse than average schools, and the attitudes of the neighbourhood may go against education, so the child may find him/herself encouraged to go out to work or even to skip school. The influence of the peer group is particularly important here.

**4   The role of the school in educational success**

(a) Good school: a well-organized school with good teaching has been shown to have significantly better results than a poorly organized school.

(b) Teachers and labelling: teachers put pupils into categories such as 'lazy' or 'chatterbox'; they then treat pupils according to these labels. Pupils respond to these labels and can have their education ruined (or improved) by these labels. One of the most important influences on a child's education appears to be the attitude of the teacher.

(c) The peer group: the class and the group of friends in which people are placed can influence their attitudes to school. Lower streams are often less keen on studying at school than the higher streams, for example. A pupil who would like to work, in a class which was basically anti-school, would find it very difficult to show his/her keenness to other classmates, for fear of ridicule.

## Gender and schooling

Girls are more successful at examinations at 16, but their numbers going on to higher level studies are lower than for boys. The subjects studied by males and females are different. Girls are more likely to study subjects in the humanities and social sciences, for example English Literature and Sociology. In sciences, the only common subjects are Biology and Human Biology. Girls are heavily under-represented in Mathematics (see figs. 2 and 3 overleaf).

The reasons for these differences include:

1 Differences in parents' treatment of boys and girls: parents have very different expectations of their sons and daughters. They also treat them differently. The education of boys is often regarded as more important than that of girls.

2 Girls and boys are bought different toys and encouraged to play different games and to have different hobbies. Boys are encouraged to play with mechanical toys and girls are encouraged to play with dolls, or to play 'nurses'.

3 In schools, teachers treat girls and boys differently, reflecting the sorts of values held by parents concerning appropriate behaviour in girls and boys. Boys are more likely to be encouraged into Science and Mathematics and girls into 'caring courses' and Domestic Sciences. This is part of the hidden curriculum.

4 The organization of the school timetable is also important. Often, subjects such as Technology and Domestic Science are run at the same time, thus forcing a divide between male and female

**Fig. 2** Girls and school exams
(*% passes awarded to girls, England and Wales, 1984*)

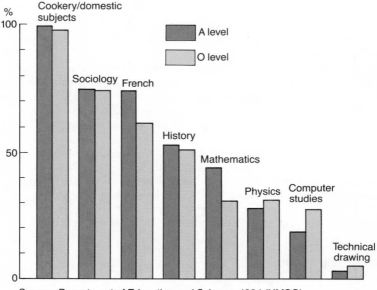

Source: *Department of Education and Science*, 1984 (HMSO)

The diagram illustrates the type of subjects chosen by girls in education. Note how few choose science/technical drawing.

subjects, as it is impossible to mix them.
**5** Peer group pressure: most girls are eager to conform to the expectations of their peer group, and this stresses attractiveness and out of school leisure activities, rather than school work.
**6** The wider culture of society: the whole culture of British society is based upon certain expectations of male and female behaviour and it is within this culture that the attitudes of teachers and parents are formed.

*Single-sex schools*
In recent years it has been suggested that co-education (mixed-sex schools) are a mistake. It is suggested that by introducing single-sex schools, girls can be offered Science and Mathematics and not see them as 'male' subjects.

Various pilot schemes such as the Girls in Science and Technology Project have created girls-only Science and Maths classes in mixed schools, with a limited degree of success. More girls took Science and Maths, but there was no major change in attitude. The reason for this is that the values of the wider culture concerning male and female behaviour intrude into the school.

**Fig. 3** What do women study at university?
(*Women as a proportion of university undergraduates*)

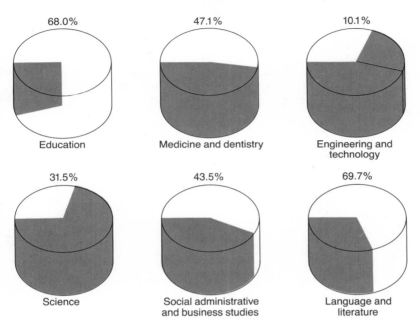

| 68.0% | 47.1% | 10.1% |
| Education | Medicine and dentistry | Engineering and technology |

| 31.5% | 43.5% | 69.7% |
| Science | Social administrative and business studies | Language and literature |

Source: *University Grants Committee*, 1984

## Ethnic minorities and education

The ethnic minorities vary in their school attainment, and it is wrong to state that they all perform badly at school. Many Indians of African origin do particularly well in our education system. Many West Indians, however, do particularly badly. The reasons for poor performance by some of the ethnic minorities include:

1 The majority of the members of the ethnic minorities are from working-class homes, and the same reasons for educational failure apply to them as to the rest of the working class.

2 Home backgrounds and inner-city neighbourhoods may not provide the same level of encouragement as do White middle-class homes.

3 The hidden curriculum: the assumptions and contents of many subjects studied at school are those of the White, European culture. Pupils are taught that British explorers 'discovered' Africa, for instance. Black people are often portrayed as stupid or inferior in books, and textbooks automatically use examples of White students. All this builds up feelings of frustration and possible inadequacy amongst Black pupils.

**4** Teacher expectations: teachers have been shown to have certain stereotyped expectations of Black pupils. For example, Tomlinson found that teachers thought that West Indians were more excitable and less academic than most children. The result is that they expect less from them, which might not give the Black pupils the encouragement other pupils receive.

**5** Language in the home: sometimes the children of immigrants talk a different form of English, or the language of their parents' countries of origin, in the home and this makes them poor writers and speakers of English at school.

**6** Racism: unfortunately, there are teachers and pupils who hold racist attitudes towards Black pupils. Indeed, racism is common in British society. Many Black pupils feel rejected and this can lead them to reject school.

*Reasons for the success of some Asian pupils*
**1** Family background: there is considerable stress in Asian homes on educational success and professional careers.
**2** Rejection of racism: the strong and distinctive Asian culture is more able to withstand British racist attitudes than the West Indian culture.
**3** Middle-class background: the children of African Asians in particular come from professional homes and therefore have the advantages of the middle class in general.

## Cultural deprivation

It has been suggested that certain groups in society are 'deprived' of the mainstream culture of British society, and therefore need extra resources. This was first suggested in The Plowden Report. As a result, the Government gives extra resources to certain inner-city areas which are seen as having special problems. This is known as positive discrimination, or compensatory education. The schools in these areas receive more equipment, there are extra teachers and they receive slightly higher rates of pay. The approach is linked to the idea of the culture of poverty (see page 122).

The idea of cultural deprivation has been criticized, because some people point out that it seems as if it presumes that the culture of immigrants is inferior to British culture. However, it is now accepted that it is important that the children of immigrants should receive extra lessons in English, as well as having some lessons taught in the language of the parents' countries of origin.

This allows the children to keep their own language and to become better in the use of English.

## Summary

**1** There are two types of learning: formal and informal. Formal learning is the type of learning which schools are organized to provide. Informal learning occurs in the casual day-to-day contact between people.
**2** The 'hidden curriculum' is the ideas and values which are passed on from teachers to pupils as part of this informal learning.
**3** The hidden curriculum covers values on such things as gender roles, attitudes to the ethnic minorities and attitudes to work.
**4** In 1944 the Butler Education Act introduced a reformed educational system, based on a meritocracy. This became known as the tripartite system.
**5** This system was criticized and comprehensive schools were introduced.
**6** Comprehensives are now being criticized in their turn, and changes to the system including city technology colleges are being suggested.
**7** There is little, if any, reliable evidence to show that comprehensives are failing to help the most able students.
**8** Certain groups do not fulfil their true potential in the education system. These groups include females, the working class and the ethnic minorities.
**9** Various explanations have been suggested, which include such things as the home, the neighbourhood, the school itself and the wider culture.

## Revision questions

1 What is the distinction between formal and informal learning? Give an example of each.
2 What is the hidden curriculum? Give one example.
3 How can the peer group influence educational success?
4 What is a 'meritocracy'?
5 Give three criticisms of comprehensives that have been made. What replies have been made by defenders of comprehensives?
6 Name any three changes in the education system that have occurred or have been seriously suggested in the 1980s.

7  Give three reasons why girls sometimes fail to fulfil their true potential at school.

8  Do all of the ethnic minorities perform badly at school? Explain your answer.

9  Explain the meaning of the term 'positive discrimination'. Give one example of it.

10  Look at fig. 1.

(a) Overall, what does fig. 1 tell you about social class and entry to university?

(b) What percentage of students in higher education comes from professional homes?

# 9  Social control and crime

## Aims of the chapter

In this chapter we will examine:

1  The meaning of types of social control.

2  The way that different societies have different forms of social control.

3  The distinctions between crime and deviance.

4  An explanation of the way that what is considered deviant varies from one situation to another.

5  The meaning and importance of labelling and stereotypes.

6  A discussion of the relationship between age/social class/gender/ethnic group and crime.

7  Why crime is more likely in inner-city areas.

8  Sociological and non-sociological explanations of crime.

9  A discussion on the reliability of official statistics of crime.

10  The meaning and importance of white-collar crime.

### Types of social control

For society to exist, there needs to be order and predictability. Socialization and social control are the means by which people are persuaded to conform to the values and behaviour of society.

**K**

*Informal control*
This is the form of social control which is experienced by people in

their daily lives, in our routine settings of home, work and school. People who act in a way not regarded as normal by the other people in these situations are 'persuaded' to conform in a number of ways. The non-conformist is spoken to, or is the subject of jokes, or, in extreme cases, is 'sent to Coventry'.

The peer group, the group of people in a similar situation, the members of which look to each other for guidance on behaviour, is particularly important in making people conform. An example of this is a group of friends, or the pupils in a particular class. People are usually very keen to conform to the peer group and not be ignored or laughed at by other members of it.

The family is a second important influence on behaviour. Again, behaviour rejected by the family is likely to influence a family member's attitudes.

*Formal control*
This is the official, legal element of social control. There are laws which guide behaviour and there are groups whose job it is to enforce these laws and rules. Those who commit crime and are found by the police are punished by the courts.

It is not just laws that are part of formal control; it is also the rules of institutions such as schools and offices. In schools there are rules which must be obeyed, and punishments for those who do not obey them.

## Social control in other societies

In British society there is great stress on formal control. In simpler societies, such as the Trobriand Islands of the Pacific, 60 years ago, there was little formal control and a much greater stress on informal control:
1  The population was small, and so personal, face-to-face control was possible.
2  People would do favours for others and this helped bind them together in mutual debt.
3  Shared religion helped to draw people together.
4  There was neither police force nor courts.

## Crime and deviance

Criminal acts are those acts which break the law, for example, robbery. Deviant acts are those which are regarded as abnormal acts by other people, for example, belching after a meal. Not all deviant acts are criminal.

Deviant acts become criminal when the majority of people

think they are serious and ought to be subject to law, or when a group of people form a pressure group and begin a campaign to make an act illegal. This may be because they believe it is evil or that it is in their interests to have the act made illegal.

*What is considered deviant varies*
The same acts are not always considered deviant, they vary according to various factors:
1 **Time** Behaviour seen as deviant at one period of history may not be considered deviant at another. Behaviour and attitudes today tend to be very different from those of Victorian England.
2 **Society** Different societies have different expectations of behaviour. In Muslim cultures women are expected to act in a far more modest way than in the main British culture.
3 **Place** Wearing a swimming costume is acceptable on the beach, not in school.
4 **Who commits the act** Behaviour by some people is acceptable, but if performed by someone else is seen as deviant. A 17-year-old in a discotheque is normal, but a 70-year-old would be thought eccentric and even deviant.

*Why definitions of deviance vary*
Individuals are defined as deviants or not depending upon:
1 How much power they have: the more power, the less chance of their actions being defined as deviant. For example, rich people who act in a peculiar way may be defined as 'eccentric', while the less well off may be termed mad.
2 How much status a person has: a person with high status may do something different and actually set a fashion.
3 Values and ideas of appropriate behaviour change over time and so an act may fit in with generally acceptable values in one period and not in another.

## Labelling and stereotypes

As we have seen, what is defined as a deviant act varies, and who is defined as deviant varies too. For those people who are labelled as deviant or criminal, there are many consequences. This is the result of being treated differently. For instance, people who are labelled as mad are often treated as if anything they do is the result of their madness. People who are labelled as criminals may be treated as if they are incapable of good actions. People who are labelled as homosexual may be regarded as incapable of talking to other males without trying to 'pick them up'. All these ideas about the labelled deviants may well be untrue. Nevertheless, once labels are placed on people, this usually has important consequences for them.

An important point to note is that people do not actually have to have committed a deviant act to be labelled as deviant. If people believe that a person is deviant in some way, then they act towards them accordingly. The police may respond in a specific way to groups who are labelled as 'troublemakers', such as young males (both Blacks and Whites), treating them differently to others.

Usually, people are labelled and treated according to **stereotypes**. For example the stereotype of a male homosexual is that he is very effeminate looking and acts like a female too. This may well not be true, but anyone who looks like this becomes labelled and treated as a homosexual by others. Stereotypes are constantly reinforced by images presented in the media; all criminals are expected to look tough and dangerous, and all football hooligans are expected to look like skinheads etc.

Patterns of crime

*Gender and crime*
Males are seven times more likely than females to commit crime, according to official statistics (see fig. 1 overleaf). Reasons include:
1 Males are brought up to be more aggressive and tougher than females. This may lead to delinquent and criminal acts.
2 Girls are more closely supervised by parents.
3 Boys who wish to rebel do so by delinquent acts, whereas girls tend to do so by sexual acts.

A criticism of this is that the official statistics of crime seriously underestimate the number of crimes performed by women. This is partly because they are more likely to be let off by police officers before coming to court.

*Age and crime*
There is a distinction between **delinquency**, which is certain types of crime committed by young people, and proper criminal acts, which are serious crimes committed mainly by older people. Most offences are committed by people under the age of 25. The older people get, the less likely they are to commit crime. The reason is that young people are not tied down by responsibilities

**Fig. 1** The guiltier sex (*Juveniles sentenced for indictable offences in 1984*)

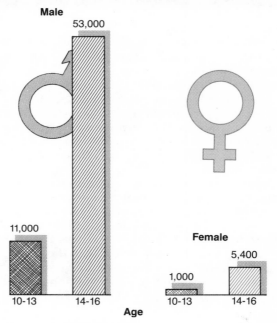

Source: *New Society*, 1986

such as a mortgage and a family to look after. They are also on the look out for excitement. They are more likely to find themselves in a situation where they have the opportunity to commit crime.

### Geographical location and crime

Most recorded crime is committed in the cities, rather than in country areas. The reasons include:
1 There is far greater poverty and social deprivation in the cities.
2 There is greater temptation and opportunity to commit crime.
3 Because of the large numbers of people, there is less informal social control.

### Social class and crime

Crime rates are much higher amongst the working class than the middle class. The reasons include:
1 In our society, there is a tremendous stress on being successful in financial terms – to possess lots of consumer goods. The working class have less opportunity to succeed legally. They are, therefore, more likely to be tempted by illegal means to be successful. This desire to be well off, even if achieved illegally, is known as anomie.

**2** Some of the working class have different values from the main ones of society, which are more favourable to committing crime. These alternative sets of values are subcultures.
**3** Working-class youths may feel bitter against society, and commit acts to get revenge to give themselves a feeling of self-importance and status. This is known as **status frustration**.

*Ethnic group and crime*
Rates of crime by those of West Indian origin are higher than average; rates of crime by Asians, however, are much lower than average. As Blacks belong disproportionately to the working class, they suffer from the same disadvantages, plus the added dimension of racism. They are more often found in the deprived inner-city areas, and the subjects of their crime are generally other Blacks, rather than Whites.

*Alternative, non-sociological explanations for criminal acts*
The explanations given for crime and delinquency above are from sociologists. Psychologists explain crime in different ways. They say that a particular type of personality may be attracted to crime. These personalities are partly the result of parental upbringing (sociologists would agree with this). However, they also say that personality is partly 'born into the person' in the sense that they inherit it biologically from their parents. (Sociologists do not agree with this; they say that both laws and individual personalities are the result of society.)

## Criminal statistics

Official statistics need to be treated with caution. Official statistics reflect the number of crimes **reported** to the police, and how they **categorize** them.

*The reporting of crimes*
People do not always report crimes to the police. They generally report crimes if they are very serious or if there is some reward in it for them – for example, when an insurance claim is to be made.
    Crimes are not reported when:
**1** People do not think it is serious.
**2** When people feel it is a private matter, between family members or friends, for example.
**3** When it would involve them in possible prosecution.
**4** When they are unable, or unaware they are the victims of crime – they may be dead!
**5** When it is humiliating, for example, rape.

*Police action*

1 The police will tend to 'pick on' certain groups, young males for example, who they think are more likely to commit crime. They therefore discover more crime among 'suspect' groups, which might pass unnoticed in other groups.

2 The police put more officers in certain areas in which they think there will be more crime. They therefore discover more crime.

3 The police in one area may be more strict on one law than other police forces, and have more prosecutions, for example, for drunken driving.

### White-collar crime

Most of the crime which the police and public see as important is 'street-crime', that is, crimes such as robbery and housebreaking. However, much more money is stolen through white-collar crime, which is crime committed by middle-class people in companies. This may involve altering a computer program to pay a person sums of money illegally, or 'fiddling the books' to avoid taxation.

There is far less public interest in this form of crime, as it is not regarded as being important or dangerous. Indeed it is often admired, for example tax evasion. The police are less likely to investigate this sort of crime, because it is often highly technical, and it is rarely reported. Companies prefer to keep quiet, as it spoils their public image if they have thieves in the management.

The laws are much weaker concerning white-collar crime. This is shown by the lack of control on the Stock Exchange, even though individuals have allegedly obtained large sums of money through unlawful dealings.

## Summary

1 Social control is necessary to ensure the continuation of society, by making life predictable and by ensuring a degree of agreement on how to behave.

2 There are two types of control: formal and informal. In many simpler societies, there was no formal control.

3 Crime refers to law-breaking behaviour. Deviance refers to all behaviour which is considered incorrect. This can include criminal behaviour.

4 Behaviour considered deviant varies by society, time, place and who commits the act.

5 Labelling is when a person or group is regarded as having particular characteristics and is treated accordingly. It does not matter if the person really does have those characteristics or not.

6 There are higher rates of crime in inner-city areas, committed by young males.

7 Females have lower rates of crime than males.

8 Explanations for the higher rates of crime amongst males and in inner-city areas include subculture and deprivation.

9 Criminal statistics must be treated with a degree of caution. Criminal acts are not always reported to the police, and much depends on how the police respond to and categorize reports of crime.

10 Police are likely to enforce the law more strongly against certain groups than others.

11 White-collar crime is crime committed by middle-class people, usually in stealing from the companies they work for. Sometimes it is the owners of companies who deliberately break the law. The punishment for white-collar crime is often lighter than for other forms of crime.

## Revision questions

1 What is the difference between formal and informal control? Give an example of each.

2 Are crime and deviance the same thing? Explain your answer and give an example of each.

3 How can it be true that an identical act can be deviant in one situation and not in another? Give an example of your own.

4 What consequences can come from being 'labelled'?

5 Why are girls likely to commit less crime than boys?

6 Why are crime rates higher for the working class than the middle class?

7 Give three reasons why people might not report a crime.

8 What is white-collar crime? Give two examples.

9 Look at fig. 1:

(a) What is the age at which males are most likely to commit crimes?

(b) What number of offences are committed by females of the same age?

# 10 Politics and power

## Aims of the chapter

In this chapter we will examine:

1 The meaning of the terms **power** and **authority**.
2 The way that power and authority influence our lives.
3 The different types of political system in the world.
4 What the major political parties in Britain stand for.
5 The influences on people's voting choices.
6 The meaning of political socialization and how it happens.
7 How opinion polls can influence voting.
8 The importance of pressure groups in a democracy, and how they achieve their aims.

### Power and authority

**K**

**Power** is when a person or a group forces other people to do what they want, for example, a kidnapper. **Authority** is when a person or group is obeyed because others believe that it is right and correct that they should be obeyed, for example, teacher and pupils.

There are three different types of authority:
1 **Charismatic** people are obeyed because they have a particular personality that people feel is awe-inspiring, for example, Jesus Christ.
2 **Traditional** people are obeyed because they have always been obeyed, for example, parents.
3 **Legal-rational** people are obeyed because they hold a particular position in an organization, for example, a manager of an office.

In reality the three types of authority are usually mixed together. In our daily lives we are constantly meeting situations of power and authority and they influence the way we act. In the family, in school, at work – all are examples of where power and authority are in action. Usually we are happy to obey when an act is seen as based upon authority, but not when it is based upon power.

**Political systems** vary too. Democracies are based upon authority, and dictatorships are based upon power; many countries rely upon soldiers and police to control the ordinary population through fear.

**Fig. 1** Authority and power in different situations

"Power and authority are happening everyday"

## Types of political system

### Democracy
This is the type of political system of Britain and Western
Europe:
1 There are free elections in which people vote to choose between
genuinely different parties.
2 There is a free press which criticizes the government and
provides information.
3 People are free to criticize the government in public and can
organize into groups to put their views forward.
4 There is an independent police and legal system.

### Totalitarianism (dictatorships)
This is the type of political system found in many parts of the
world – for example, in Eastern Europe and certain states in
South America and Africa:
1 The country is controlled by a small group (an élite) for their

benefit, or in accordance with that group's views.
2 Broadcasting and the press are State controlled.
3 People are not allowed to express their views.
4 There are no genuine elections.
5 The police and legal system are directly controlled by the government, to its benefit.

## British political parties

1 **Labour** This is a socialist party which stresses the need for profits of big business to be shared among the people through government action.
2 **Conservative** This is the party that believes that governments ought to create an environment for business to do well, and that people should be encouraged to look after themselves.
3 **Liberal** This party sees itself as more caring than the Conservatives, yet not as radical as Labour.
4 **Social Democratic** Formed by breakaway MPs from the Labour Party as they thought it was too left-wing.

## Voting behaviour

The way people vote is influenced by:
1 Their social class.
2 Their image of what the political parties stand for.
3 Their geographical location.
4 Their ethnic group.
5 Age and gender.

### K  *Social class*

Until the 1970s the most important influence without any doubt was a person's social-class background. Until then, it was a fact that two thirds of the working class voted Labour and three fifths of the middle class voted Conservative.

This is not true today, for the following reasons:
1 The division of the working class between the 'traditional' working class, who have the less well-paid jobs and live in rented council housing, and the 'new' affluent working class, who are home-owners and have had a general rise in their standard of living.
2 The success of the Conservative Party in obtaining working class votes, and the division of opposition to the Conservatives between the Labour Party and the Alliance.
3 The image of the Labour Party as being dominated by extreme left-wingers.

These factors have all combined to make the better-off working class less attached to the Labour Party.

The **division** of the working class is particularly important, as much of Labour Party policy has been aimed at a section of the working class – the traditional working class – which is rapidly shrinking in size.

### Party images
The Labour Party is seen to be the party of the traditional working class and is associated with government intervention. The Conservative policy is associated with individual 'freedom', the middle class and business interests. The SDP is seen as a less radical version of the Labour Party. The Liberal Party has an image of being caring. People are influenced by these images, which in part are created by the press, even if they are not true.

### Geographical location
The Conservative Party gains the majority of its seats from the south of England and the Labour Party from the north of Britain. Also, the city centres are more likely to be Labour, while the suburbs are more likely to vote Conservative or SDP. Country areas vote Conservative and Liberal.

These voting divisions reflect differences in the income and social class of the people living in these areas. For example, people living in the suburbs are more likely to be better off and to see the image of the Conservative Party as one for them.

### Ethnic group
The ethnic minorities are more likely to vote Labour than for any other party, partly because they are more likely to be working class and because it is commonly believed that Labour takes a greater interest in the problems of the ethnic minorities.

### Age and gender
Before the 1970s, these factors were regarded as important, but today they have declined in importance. There is little evidence to show that people become politically more conservative as they grow older. Women are more likely to vote SDP than Labour but otherwise there is little difference between the sexes.

Figure 2 overleaf illustrates some of the influences on the voter.

Political socialization

People learn political attitudes just like any other set of ideas in

**Fig. 2** Influences on the voter

Ethnic group

Social class

Geographical location

Age & gender

Political socialization

Party images

Conservative

Liberal   SDP

Labour

K

the process of socialization. In particular, the following are important:

**1 The family** Parents' attitudes are a powerful influence on young people, and may remain throughout a person's life.

**2 The television and newspapers** Though there is no evidence to show that these influence voting behaviour directly, they do create a general feeling and attitude towards political events.

**3 The peer group** The attitudes of people with whom we mix may influence us, particularly if we admire their style of life and aspire to be like them.

### Opinion polls

K

Opinion polls are surveys which ask people their voting intentions. They are regularly published in newspapers. They are generally very accurate. The accuracy of the polls depends upon:

**1** How typical of the population the people asked are – the worse the sample, the greater the inaccuracy.

**2** The closeness to an election: the nearer the election, the greater the accuracy – as people are more likely to have made up their minds.

**3** The truthfulness of the replies people give.

*The influence of opinion polls on voters*
In some European countries, such as France and West Germany, opinion polls are banned before elections. The reason is that the results of opinion polls can influence the way people vote.
**1** If opinion polls suggest a large majority for one party, then people who would have voted for that party may not bother to vote. This may actually make the favourite party lose.
**2** Alternatively, people may switch their vote to the weaker party to make sure that the majority of the winning party is not too great.
**3** If polls suggest that a particular party is only just losing, then people may abandon other political parties to try to edge the party which is just losing to victory. It has been suggested that this has benefited the Liberals and SDP in Britain.
**4** Politicians are influenced by opinion polls too, and may alter their policies in order to remain in favour with the electorate. This may not result in the best policies, just the most popular.

## Pressure groups

Pressure groups (sometimes known as interest groups) are organizations formed by people who want to persuade those in power to adopt their ideas. Pressure groups vary from ones concerned with the protection of animals, right through to those protesting about nuclear weapons.
The difference between a pressure group and a political party is that pressure groups are concerned only with single, particular issues. Pressure groups do not put up candidates for election. Political parties are concerned with a broad range of policies and they put up candidates for elections.

*Types of pressure group*
**1 Promotional groups**, which put forward a viewpoint that they believe is good for the community and does not simply benefit themselves. An example would be the Friends of the Earth, who are concerned with such things as pollution and conservation.
**2 Protective or defensive groups**, which are concerned with looking after their own interests. An example is the Automobile Association, which looks after the interests of car drivers.

*The importance of pressure groups in a democracy*
Without pressure groups, democracies would not be as representative of the people as they are. Political parties are

organizations which contain within them very broad ranges of interests. They cannot reflect the wide varieties of political and social opinion that the whole population have. Pressure groups are concerned with single issues, which often cut across party lines. For example, there are no party viewpoints on hanging or abortion, these are left to the conscience of individual MPs. Pressure groups pull together the supporters of a particular policy and they then press decision-makers to adopt their views. Pressure groups are extremely important in helping the politicians keep 'in touch' with the people.

1 As political parties represent a broad range of opinions, they often do not have policies on particular issues. Pressure groups allow people to have specific viewpoints represented.

2 Pressure groups keep the Government informed, between elections, of the wishes of the people on particular issues.

*How pressure groups operate*

K ▶

Pressure groups have a number of ways of influencing decision-makers.

1 Pressure groups may employ MPs or pay their expenses.

2 Pressure groups may organize campaigns to publicize their causes.

3 Pressure groups may provide information to decision-makers, which would otherwise be unknown.

4 Pressure groups may organize demonstrations and rallies.

5 If all else fails pressure groups may use illegal methods such as obstruction and even sabotage and arson, as in the case of the Animal Liberation Front.

Figure 3 illustrates the role of pressure groups.

## Summary

1 People can get others to do what they want by either power or authority.

2 Power and authority are not just used in politics, but in everyday life.

3 There are a number of different political systems in the world, but the main division is between democracies and dictatorships.

4 People are influenced in their voting by a number of factors, including class, party image, ethnic group and geographical location.

5 Political socialization is the process of learning about politics and having political attitudes. It is influenced by the media and

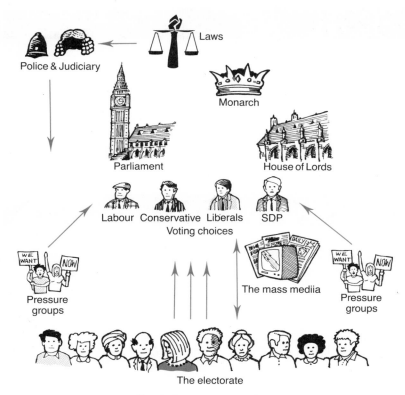

**Fig. 3** Democracy in action

the family, as well as by the peer group.

**6** Pressure groups are organizations which try to persuade those in power to adopt a particular viewpoint of which they are in favour. They are interested in single issues, and do not wish to put forward candidates in elections. They are, therefore, different from political parties.

**7** Pressure groups are very important in democracies because they keep the Government in touch with the opinions of the people.

**8** Pressure groups operate in a wide number of ways outside Parliament to persuade MPs to listen to them. Their methods include: publicity, demonstrations, research activities.

## Revision questions

**1** Briefly explain the difference between power and authority.
**2** Give three differences between democracy and dictatorship.
**3** Give three influences that affect voting choices.

4   Why have some countries banned opinion polls?
5   What differences are there between a pressure group and a political party?
6   Describe two ways a pressure group can persuade those in power to take their viewpoint.
7   Why are pressure groups important in a democracy?

# 11   Population

## Aims of the chapter

In this chapter we will examine:

1   How information about population change is obtained.
2   The importance of gaining information on changes in the population.
3   What factors determine the size of the country's population.
4   What changes have taken place in the birth rate, and the reasons for these.
5   The changes in the death rate and the reasons for these.
6   The balance of the sexes.
7   The fact that people are living longer and the consequences of this.
8   The way that the distribution of the population over the country is changing.

### Demography

This means the study of changes in the population.

*How information is collected on the population*

1   The most important means of collecting information is the census. This is a form that every household must complete every ten years. The census asks questions about the amenities (toilets, kitchens, number of bedrooms, etc.) a household has, and the number of people in that household.
2   The second main method of finding information is the registry of births, marriages and deaths. Every birth, marriage and death must be recorded in an office of the local authority. This information is then collected nationally and gives an excellent picture of the changing population.

*The importance of demography*
A detailed study of the population is absolutely crucial if the Government is to plan ahead and provide all the services that are necessary, for example:
1 **Education** By knowing the numbers of children born in any one year, the Government is able to plan the number of school places and the number of teachers needed.
2 **Housing/town planning** Typical family sizes can tell planners the numbers and types of houses that are needed.
3 **Health** The age and sex of the population can influence decisions over the sorts of service to be provided. If there are large numbers of young women, then maternity wards; if large numbers of elderly people, then special 'geriatric' wards.

## Population size

The size of the population of a country is a result of:
1 The difference between the number of people born in any one period and the number of people dying in that period (known as the **natural change** in the population).
2 The difference between the number of people emigrating (leaving the country) and those immigrating (coming in to the country).
   In Britain today there is a low birth rate, a low death rate and more people are emigrating than entering the country. The result of these things is that the population of Britain is not increasing in size and there is an increase in the proportion of the elderly.

## The birth rate

The birth rate is the number of births for every 1000 people in the population. The higher the birth rate the greater the number of children being born. The fertility rate is the number of babies being born alive for every 1000 women who are of an age capable of bearing children (about 16 – 40 years of age).

*Changes in the birth rate*
Before the beginning of the Industrial Revolution (about 1760), the British population grew very slowly indeed. The numbers of births and deaths were almost equal. However, the improvements in health and standards of living brought by industrialization meant that many more children survived their first year; this caused a population explosion. Overall in this century there has been a decline in the birth rate. This has been particularly noticeable since 1967. This decline has been caused by:

**Fig 1** The numbers of births and deaths in Britain this century
(*Note that the natural increase is the difference between births and deaths*)

Source: *Social Trends,* 1986 (HMSO)

**1** The increasing knowledge and use of contraceptives: the use of contraceptives was limited at the beginning of the century to the upper middle class. However, gradually in the last 90 years there has been a spread in the use of contraceptives to all social classes.
**2** The cost of having children has meant that people are more reluctant to have large families, preferring instead to have a high standard of living for themselves.
**3** There has been a change in the cultural expectations of society regarding family size. It has become 'normal' to have only two children.
**4** Women's attitudes to life have changed. They reject the idea that they should spend most of their lives having children. Instead they prefer a career of their own and their independence.
　However, the birth rate rose in 1919 – 21, 1945 – 8 and 1957 – 66. This was because:
**1** 1919 – 21: after World War I, the soldiers returned from the war anxious to start families.
**2** 1945 – 8: again the return of soldiers from a war increased the number of births.
**3** 1957 – 66: this was a period in which it was fashionable to marry young and to have children. There was a high standard of living and so people were able to afford to have large families. Also the children of the 'baby boom' of 1945 – 8 were coming of age to have children of their own.
　It is important to realize that for the last 10 years family size has dropped to its lowest ever. Today, the British population is

actually falling, and the average number of children in families is only 1.9.

*Social class and family size*
Family size has always varied by social class. Traditionally, the working class have had larger families than the middle class (though this is not true today). Historically, this was because the middle class this century started to use contraceptives earlier, middle-class women demanded the right to have fewer children and a life of their own earlier, and the values of the middle class laid less stress on having a large family.

## The death rate

The death rate is measured as the number of deaths per 1000 people in the population. Overall, the death rate has declined considerably in the last 150 years. This has been achieved by:
1 **Improvements in public health** Modern sewerage and refuse collection systems, as well as the provision of clean drinking water, have raised the standards of public cleanliness and wiped out killer diseases such as cholera and typhoid.
2 **Advances in medicine** Standards of health care have improved. Modern hospitals, drugs and surgical techniques have all combined to lower the chances of dying of illness.
3 **The higher standard of living** The increase in people's incomes has led to better diets, to warmer, more comfortable housing and to an overall increase in comforts. These have made people more resistant to illness.
    The result of the decline in the death rate has been to increase the length of people's lives. In turn this has meant that an increasing proportion of the population is elderly.

*The infant mortality rate*
Part of the death rate is taken up by the infant mortality rate, which means the number of deaths of babies under one year old per 1000 babies born alive. The infant mortality rate has dropped sharply this century. Reasons for this decline include all the points mentioned above with regard to the general death rate, plus:
1 **A higher standard of medical care for childbirth** The introduction of the National Health Service in the late 1940s meant that there were much better facilities for childbirth and care of the mothers. Today, there is a wide variety of clinics and special services for mothers. This has resulted in healthier mothers and babies.

**2 Sex differences** Boys have a higher infant mortality rate than girls. This is because male babies are generally weaker than female ones. In the past far more boys would have died.

**3 Social-class differences** There are still social-class differences in infant mortality. The children of upper-middle-class parents are half as likely as lower-working-class babies to die in their first year. This is because:

(a) Working-class mothers will have worse diets, and so be weaker.

(b) Working-class mothers are more likely to smoke.

(c) Working-class mothers are less likely to give (or be able to give) the highest standards of infant care.

### Patterns of migration

Migration is the movement of people from one area or country to another. Immigration is when people move into an area; emigration is when people move out.

Historically, more people have left Britain than entered it. In the 1950s and early 1960s, there was an increase in immigration, because there were so many jobs available that people already here could not fill them. Some employers encouraged people to come here from India and the West Indies. Today, there is a very low level of immigration into Britain, and slightly more people leave than enter the country. This means that there is a net loss of people through migration. The single largest immigrant group in Britain are the Irish.

### Gender and population

Sociologists are interested in the balance of the sexes in the population. There are more males up to the age of 50 than females, and more females over 50 than males. This is because:

**1** Males are more likely to die at each age than females, so the number of males gradually decreases.

**2** In the past, male babies were more likely to die than female ones, yet as more male babies are born, the numbers surviving were roughly equal. Improvements in medical facilities for child birth in the last 50 years mean that these boys now survive.

### Age and population

In 1902, 6 per cent of the population were over retirement age. Today, 15 per cent are. This means that there are fewer young people and more old people in proportion in the population. It has been described as an ageing population.

**Fig. 2** The growing numbers of the elderly    103

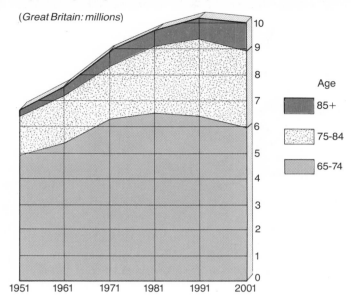

(*Great Britain: millions*)

Age
- 85+
- 75-84
- 65-74

1951  1961  1971  1981  1991  2001

Source: *New Society*, 1986

People live longer because of:
1 Improved medical services.
2 Higher standards of living which allow better diets, better housing, safer and more comfortable lives.

*Gender differences*
Women are more likely to live longer than men – by an average of six years. Women live longer because:
1 They are less likely to work in dangerous occupations, such as mining and construction and chemicals.
2 Men smoke and drink more heavily than women. This is related to cancer and heart disease.
3 Men are more likely to die in car and motorbike accidents.
The consequences of an ageing population are:
1 The burden of dependency: the retired cost a great deal in pensions and health services, which must be paid for by the rest of the working population.
2 There has to be much greater provision of medical care and social services.
3 Families are increasingly likely to have aged relatives to look after. This usually means that daughters have to shoulder this burden.

**4** Poverty for the elderly is common, as many only have State pensions to live on.
**5** The elderly become isolated as their friends and relatives die, so they are lonely.

 **K** The distribution of the population

The geographical distribution of the population is the way in which people are distributed in areas in the country and in the towns and countryside:
**1** Increasingly, people are living in the south-east.
**2** There has been a decrease in the numbers living in Scotland, the north and Wales.
**3** This is caused by the lack of jobs in these areas, and the better prospects in the south-east.
**4** There is a movement away from large towns and cities to smaller towns and to the countryside. This move away from cities and urban areas is known as **de-urbanization**.

## Summary

**1** The study of population is known as demography.
**2** Information is collected using the census and the registry of births, marriages and deaths.
**3** Demographic information is useful because it allows the Government to plan ahead.
**4** Population is determined by:
(a) the number of births,
(b) the number of deaths,
(c) the difference between the number of people leaving and entering the country to live, over a period of time.
**5** The birth rate is very low in Britain at the moment, as people usually have small families.
**6** The reasons for the low birth rate include the increasing use of contraceptives, the desire for higher living standards and the rejection of the child-rearing role by women.
**7** The death rate has declined. This is because people are living longer and the infant mortality rate has declined.
**8** There has been a large growth in the number of elderly in the population. This could lead to problems of providing adequate social services, etc.
**9** The balance of the distribution of the population is shifting towards the south-east and East Anglia. This is linked to the employment opportunities in the south.

## Revision questions

1 Why is it necessary to collect information on the changes in the population? Give two examples.
2 Briefly outline the change in the birth rate this century.
3 Is the availability of contraception the only explanation for these changes?
4 Why has the death rate declined?
5 What problems face old people, as a result of the increase in life expectancy?
6 Why do women live longer than men?
7 How is the distribution of population changing in Britain. What reasons can you suggest for this?
8 Look at fig. 1.
(a) How many births were there in 1961?
(b) What is projected to happen to the birth rate after 1991?

# 12 Age

## Aims of the chapter

In this chapter we will examine:

1 The way that age is socially constructed.
2 The way that ideas of childhood have changed over time and society.
3 How males and females are treated differently in childhood.
4 What youth culture is.
5 How youth culture started.
6 The varieties of youth culture that exist.
7 The reasons why different youth cultures emerged.
8 The effect of unemployment on youth culture.
9 The importance of the peer group.
10 The way that the elderly are viewed in British society.
11 A comparison of attitudes to the elderly in other societies.

### The social construction of age

Age is not just a physical thing, it is also social. People are expected to behave in certain ways which are seen as appropriate for their age. Most of the expected behaviour is not related to any biological process of age at all. Indeed, the expectations of age groups vary across societies and periods of history, indicating that the expectations of behaviour cannot be natural (otherwise the behaviour of people of particular ages would always be the same).

Three of the ages of particular interest to sociologists are childhood, youth and old age.

## Childhood

The idea of childhood as we know it today includes the ideas that children are immature and helpless, and need sheltering from 'unpleasant' things, such as sex.

This idea is a recent development in history. Before the 18th century most children were treated as little adults and they were expected to take on many burdens and to work. Children generally wore the same clothes as adults, and both adults and children played games (such as spinning tops). Games were not seen as being especially for the young.

The lives of young children varied by social class; it was only long after middle-class children were treated differently from adults, that the working class finally regarded children as special little creatures in need of love and attention.

The changing attitudes to childhood were reflected by the development of legislation to protect children, such as the Factory Acts of the 19th century, and in the development of schooling for children, which gradually extended from covering those up to 10 years of age, to today's minimum age of 16.

### *Childhood in other societies*

In other societies, there are very different attitudes to children. In many of the Far Eastern countries (e.g. Thailand), young children are expected to have full-time employment and it is common for girls below the age of 13 to work as prostitutes. Ideas of innocence and purity are not applied to young people in the cities of these countries.

A second example of how differently children are treated comes from a study by Colin Turnbull of life among a tribe called the Ik. Here, children were thrown out of home and expected to look after themselves, at the age of three. As a result, children banded together in order to survive. This banding together in groups also occurs in the cities of Colombia, and elsewhere in South America.

*Gender differences in childhood*
It is in childhood that the differences in behaviour we associate
with males and females are learnt.
    In the home:
1  Parents treat girls and boys differently.
2  Boys are not expected to do household jobs such as washing the
dishes.
3  Boys and girls are given different sorts of toys and are
encouraged to play different games.
4  Parents are stricter in their control of girls, especially
concerning sexual matters.
    At school:
1  Teachers act differently towards girls and boys.
2  Boys are more likely to take up Maths and sciences.
3  Girls are more likely to follow arts and social science subjects.
    In the wider society, the media treat males and females
differently in the way that they present stories and pictures.

## Youth culture

*Rites of passage*
In most societies people are divided into distinct age groups – for
example, childhood and adulthood. In order to mark publicly the
change from one age group to another, most societies have very
clear rites of passage, which are special ceremonies people
undergo. At the end of the ceremony, everyone knows that the
person has now changed age groups. Examples of rites of passage
include the 18th-birthday party, the Jewish Bar Mitzvah and,
much later in life, the retirement party.

*The origins of youth subcultures*
In Britain today, unlike previous societies, there is no clear age at
which people move from being children to being adults. This is
partly because there is no clearcut rite of passage. The result is
that people go through a long period (probably you are going
through it yourself) in which they neither see themselves as
adults, nor as children. Instead they see themselves in the 'halfway' stage of being a youth.
    What is distinctive about youth is that many of the values and
much of the behaviour of people of this age group are very
different from those of older people. This is not natural, but is as
a result of changes in society.
    There are two views on the nature of youth culture and its
origins.

**Fig. 1** The changing face of youth culture

| The Merry-Go-Round of Style | | | |
|---|---|---|---|
| *Styles* | *Words* | *Artefacts* | *Pastimes* |
| **1950s** | | | |
| Polo-neck sweaters, Brylcreem, busts, Beatnik, duffel coats. Festival of Britain | Cool, hip, supersonic, dig-it | Hula-hoops, yo-yos, bubble cars, horror comics, roller skates | Coffee bars, ten-pin bowling, tearing cinema seats, National Service, jiving, the twist |
| **1960s** | | | |
| Mods, miniskirts, hippies, kipper ties, hipsters, chelsea boots, chisel-toes | Fab, groovy, square, with-it, 'man', swinging, wow | Tower blocks, ring roads, hovercraft, scooters, colour supplements, universities | Bingo, demos, ten-pin bowling, cannabis, LSD, squatting |
| **1970s** | | | |
| Stripped pine, Habitat, pop, punk, skinhead, vests, hot pants, afro hair | Right-on, way-out, triffic, super, pigs, too much | Breathalysers, double-glazing, pedestrian precincts, skateboards, trannies, training shoes, QE2, Concorde | Pop festivals, graffiti, real ale, heart transplants, diy, streaking, cohabitation |
| **1980s** | | | |
| Short hair, gay, Sloane Ranger, New Romantic, high tech, Laura Ashley | Laid back, no-way, brill, naff, wally | Digital watches, personal computers, Walkman radios, bmx bikes | Jogging, cocktails, fast food, glue sniffing, video nasties, cocaine/heroin |

Source: *New Society,* 1984

**1 The single youth culture view** This approach stresses the fact that youth culture is a set of values which most young people share as a result of having to cope with the problems of changing from a child to an adult and becoming independent of their family. According to this view, young people develop a similar culture, separate from their parents, which gives them a feeling of security and independence. The values of youth culture allow them to rebel against their parents and to be independent.

**2 Youth culture as an umbrella term** This approach to youth culture points out the wide varieties of youth cutural 'styles' that exist ('Gothics', 'casuals', 'alternative', etc.). If youth culture was simply a form of rebellion against adults, then presumably all young people would adopt a similar style of fashion. The reason why this is not so, according to many sociologists, is that the great differences between young people (ethnic group, social class, gender) are reflected in the youth culture that they choose.

(a) **Middle-class youth culture**: stresses the 'student protest' type of behaviour and style. This reflects the longer period in education.

(b) **Working-class youth cultures**: these stress the response of working-class young people to their futures, which may well consist of boring, fairly low-paid work, or unemployment. The styles adopted by the working class stress getting the most out of life and having fun. The styles also reflect many of the values which belong in the working-class culture generally. So often (as was the case with skinheads and today with casuals), the stress is on being tough and manly.

(c) **Black youth culture**: this is very similar to the youth culture of the working-class youth. This is not surprising, as most Blacks are working class. However, there is a great deal of racism in Britain and Blacks often feel rejected. The adoption of 'Rastafarianism' by young Blacks shows a desire to have a distinct culture of their own which is not 'borrowed' from White working-class culture.

(d) **Asian youth culture**: this has been the slowest group to develop a separate youth culture. This is probably because the strict family life of Asians and the self-contained nature of the community means that there is little chance for Asian youth to develop their own styles, distinct from parents.

(e) **Girls in youth culture**: there is a clear difference between the behaviour of males and females in youth culture. It seems that for females, their freedom is far more limited than that of males and that they are not expected to be as sexually active as males. The stress of female youth is on being attractive to males and of having a boyfriend. Girls are less likely to play a central part in mixed-sex youth groups.

*The peer group*
A peer group is a group of people usually of the same age, with whom a person compares his or her behaviour. These might be friends in school or those who share similar attitudes to fashion and music. The influence of the peer group is very important and young people can 'drift' into delinquency, drug use, or any particular form of behaviour, if they feel that is how other members of their peer group expect them to behave.

*Unemployment and youth culture*
In the last 10 years the level of youth unemployment has increased massively. The result is that the affluence (having a lot of money to spend) that initially started youth culture in Britain is declining among young people. In some inner-city areas the level of youth employment is around 50 per cent. This is influencing the way in which youth behave.

**1 A rise in the crime rates** Youth now have high expectations of the sorts of consumer goods to expect (such as stereos and smart clothes) compared to earlier generations. However, as there are so few jobs, they are unable to buy these things. It is possible that as expectations remain high, this is encouraging a rise in juvenile crime.

**2 Conflict with the police and inner-city riots** The lack of jobs and the high material expectations of young people have led them in to conflict with the police, and have created a very tense climate in the inner cities.

Today's youth are likely to hang around city centres, as a way of passing the time mainly, but this can appear threatening to some of the older generation and to shopkeepers. The result is that the police are increasingly called in to control youth, giving them the impression of being 'picked on'.

**3  A sense of hopelessness** For working-class youth, the traditional escape route from the home was the purchase of a car and later the ability to afford to marry and have a separate home of one's own. Lack of jobs is forcing youth to remain at home longer and to be dependent on their parents. This results in a feeling of frustration amongst youth and conflict within the family.

Against these points, for the first few years after leaving school, most youth have little resentment as they receive State benefit, are free to do what they like and have no sense of themselves as workers (unlike their parents), so they do not 'miss' work.

*The generation gap*
It is often claimed that there is a generation gap between youth and the older generation. A *New Society* survey in 1986 found little evidence to support this. Most young people have similar values to their parents, and friction with them is over fairly unimportant matters such as styles of dress.

## The elderly

There have never been so many people over retirement age alive. In modern British society, the position of the elderly and our attitudes towards them have changed considerably:
1  The elderly are often viewed as a 'burden' to be looked after.
2  This is strengthened by the fact that people have to retire at the age of 60 or 65, whether they wish to or not.
3  The elderly are costly in medical care and pensions.
4  The elderly have very low status.
5  The elderly are not seen as having much to contribute in the way of knowledge or skill.

The elderly in other cultures are treated very differently. For example among Asians in Britain, the elderly are regarded as being the heads of the household and are treated with great respect. Their views are important and they often still have jobs to do in family businesses. In Japan too, the elderly are treated with great respect and are not ignored simply because they are old.

## Summary

1  Age is a social creation as much as a biological one. Different behaviour of the various age groups is the result of social expectations, rather than a reflection of natural abilities.
2  The modern British idea of childhood is very different from that in other societies and in Britain in the past. We treat children as innocent little creatures in need of care and protection. In other societies, and in the past in Britain, they were treated more as 'little' adults.
3  Rites of passage are ceremonies which mark the passing of an individual from one status (for example, childhood) to another (for example, adulthood).
4  In Britain there is no rite of passage which clearly marks the move into adulthood. Partly as a result, youth has developed.
5  Youth culture is the values and attitudes which youth hold at any particular time which makes their behaviour different from that of older people.
6  There are two views on the nature of youth culture. One group of sociologists argues that there is one shared youth culture, and the other group argues that there are really a wide variety of youth cultures, reflecting gender, race and class differences.
7  The peer group is a very important influence on the behaviour of young people. A peer group consists of people of the same age who influence each other's behaviour.
8  Unemployment has had a considerable effect on the behaviour of youth. There is a belief that it has led to more crime, for instance.
9  There is a continuing increase in the numbers of elderly people in Britain. In Britain older people have low status, but this is not true in other societies, such as Japan, where old people are valued for their experience of life.

## Revision questions

1  Explain why age is not just a physical thing, but also 'social'.
2  Is the way that we treat children in British society today 'natural'? Explain your answer.
3  What is a 'rite of passage'? Give two examples.
4  Why is it wrong to say that there is only one youth culture?
5  Take one youth culture (or style) and suggest reasons for its existence.
6  What is a 'peer group'?

7 Suggest how rising unemployment may affect youth.
8 Compare attitudes to the elderly amongst the British Asian community to those of the majority of British society.

## 13 Mass media

### Aims of the chapter

In this chapter we will examine:

1 The way that the mass media are different from face-to-face communication.
2 The power of the media to stereotype certain groups and the consequences this has for those groups.
3 The explanations of the mass media's influence on our behaviour.
4 The patterns of ownership and control.
5 How the newspapers choose their contents and the importance of these choices.
6 The way that the record industry 'packages' music.

### Types of mass media

1 The mass media (the word is plural) are all the ways of communicating from a single source to a large number (a 'mass') of people. This includes such things as newspapers, television, radio, cinema, recordings and videos.
2 The audience has little chance of replying to the mass media, as the communication is one way.
3 The mass media provide news or entertainment to a pre-arranged formula, for example in half-hour slots on television, or in a certain number of pages in a newspaper.
4 The mass media are generally run for a profit (but not in the case of the BBC).
5 The mass media are based on advanced technology.
   This contrasts with normal face-to-face interaction:
1 This is directly between people.
2 It involves an exchange of ideas.
3 It is not fixed or scheduled in length or format.
4 Usually, it is not conducted with advanced technology (telephones are an exception).

**Fig. 1** The importance of television in our lives – a comparison by social class and sex

Average weekly hours viewed per person by sex and social class

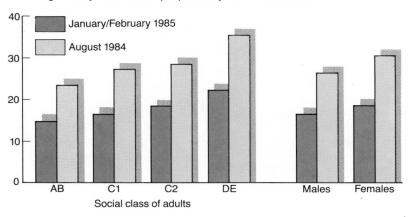

Source: *New Society,* 1986

## The mass media and stereotyping

The mass media provide the majority of people with their
knowledge about the world beyond their personal experiences,
and with a set of attitudes. The media are very powerful,
therefore. One of the things that the media do is to **label** certain
groups in a particular way and then to create **stereotypes** about
them. These labels then influence the way people treat the
particular group.

A label is a particular description or name that we link to
certain patterns of behaviour, for example, thief, chatterbox,
sexy, loud-mouthed. A stereotype is a whole batch of ideas and
expectations and images of behaviour, styles of dress and
language associated with particular groups. For example, the
stereotype of a doctor is male, middle aged, middle class, well
dressed with no regional accent.

Here are some examples of the way that the media label and
stereotype certain groups.

### Youth

Young people are often portrayed in a negative light by the media
and it would sometimes seem as if all youth are members of
extreme fashion cults, or engaged in crime, football hooliganism
or drug-taking. The reason why they are shown as being so

extreme in the newspapers is that excitement, sex and crime attract viewers' and readers' interest.

One very famous study of the relationship between the media and youth was done in the 1960s by Stanley Cohen, who studied 'mods' and 'rockers'. He found that the mass media helped to create the fashion of mods and rockers, and then constructed stories which created a stereotype of these two groups as violent rivals, always fighting. This led to young people identifying themselves as mods or rockers, seeing violence as appropriate behaviour to adopt, and going out to fight each other. The police in turn had a stereotyped image of every person who dressed in the fashions of mod or rocker and assumed they were out looking for trouble, and tended to treat them accordingly. Had there been less sensationalization in the papers, there may not have been as much trouble

Similar sorts of argument have been put forward to explain the outbreaks of football hooliganism, and even the inner-city riots of the 1980s.

*Women*
Women are portrayed very differently to men, in the media. *The Sun* prints a photograph of a 'pin-up' every day, and even in ordinary news stories, the newspapers think it relevant to give the age and attractiveness of most women interviewed. Women tend to be placed into two main categories, that of sexiness, and that of the caring figure. This leads to an image of what women are like naturally, and how they ought to behave. Women who do not fit the stereotypes are therefore regarded as 'odd'.

Explanations of mass media influence on our behaviour

Most people believe that the mass media influence our behaviour in certain ways, but are not quite sure how this is. Explanations include:

**The behaviourist (or 'hypodermic syringe') model** This explanation suggests that people are attracted to violent or sexually exciting material in the media, and are then influenced to try out that behaviour themselves.

**The audience selection model** This model suggests that people are very selective in their reading and viewing, and that they take out of things only the information that suits them. People then forget or ignore the rest. In this view, the media only reinforce ideas and values that people have anyway.

**The cultural approach** This model goes slightly further than

**Fig. 2** Ownership of the Press                                                    115

Who owns what?

The big five newspaper proprietors (with foundation dates of newspapers)

Pergamon Press

Daily Mirror (1903)

Sunday Mirror (1963)

Sunday People (1881)

**Fleet Holdings**

Daily Express (1900)

Daily Star (1978)

Sunday Express (1918)

Associated Newspapers Group

Daily Mail (1896)

Mail on Sunday (1982)

**News International**

The Sun (1964)

The Times (1785)

News of the World (1843)

Sunday Times (1822)

Telegraph Newspaper Trust

Daily Telegraph (1855)

Sunday Telegraph (1961)

Source: *New Society*, 1986

the audience selection model. It argues that any influence of the media will be long term, gradually changing the whole climate of opinion on certain matters. The media do not have an immediate and direct influence, instead they act slowly, over a long time.

*An example of the influence of the media: violence*
Many people blame the media for encouraging people to violence, although there is little direct evidence that the media encourage people to commit violent acts. However, the media do seem to reinforce attitudes already held by some people who are attracted to violence anyway. The media are not the cause of violence, they simply strengthen the attitudes of those who are attracted to violence.

It is important to remember that the media comprise only one of a number of agencies which help to socialize us. There are also the family, the school, the legal system, religion and the workplace. The outcome of our actions is a result of the mix of all of these.

**K** ▶ *An example of the influence of the media: voting behaviour*
A second area of discussion has been the influence of the media on people's voting patterns.

It has been suggested that effective use of the media by the Conservative Party in recent years has won them many votes. However, research indicates that people do not switch their votes as a result of newspaper or television reporting, at least in the short term. As we saw earlier, people tend to choose the information that they want, and ignore other pieces of information that do not fit in with the views they already hold. What may happen, though, is that over a long period, newspapers and television reporting of events 'sets the agenda', that is, creates a climate of opinion which in the long term can affect attitudes to politics. As most newspapers are supporters of the Conservative Party, this suggests that the influence of newspapers has been to create a 'climate of opinion' favourable to Conservative views on politics.

Ownership and control of the media

*Ownership*
The media are owned by relatively few companies. The top five companies in newspaper publishing control 90 per cent of sales, for example. Television is dominated by five commercial companies plus the BBC, and in book publishing, the top five companies take a very large proportion of sales. There is a move towards fewer and fewer companies dominating the market, as take-overs occur.

*Control*
The few companies that dominate the market in television, publishing and newspapers are themselves owned by very few people. Two men alone, Rupert Murdoch and Robert Maxwell, have effective control of about 70 per cent of daily newspapers sold. It has been argued, therefore, that these men directly control the contents of the newspapers, putting in them what they want. However, this does not seem to be entirely the case:
1 The newspapers must sell profitably, so they have to attract readers.

**2** The newspapers must also attract advertisers.
**3** In broadcasting, the commercial companies have a regulating body – the IBA – which is responsible for standards, whilst the BBC has an independent Board of Governors.

## Newspapers

Newspapers vary to an extent in what they choose to include and the way they present their contents.
**1** There are two types of paper:
(a) **Tabloids**, which are the smaller, mass market papers, such as *The Daily Mirror, The Sun* and *The Daily Mail*. These papers include mainly articles and photographs on gossip, scandal and sport.
(b) **The quality papers**, which include *The Guardian* and *The Daily Telegraph*. These include heaver articles on politics, economics and social events.
**2** Newspapers vary in their contents, as they try to appeal to different readers and to be as popular as possible to the particular group they have chosen. The quality papers aim at the better educated, middle-class market. The tabloids aim at the majority of people who are not particularly interested in politics. Figure 3 gives details of newspaper readership by social class.
**3** Newspapers need to appeal to advertisers. In order to do this, they must prove that they are popular with the sorts of people that the advertisers want. So, the newspapers must sell enough copies to survive and enough copies to the right sort of person.
**4** Journalistic values are important too. Journalists receive huge amounts of information, and they must decide what is to be included in the papers and what importance it is to be given:
(a) Importance: the action reported must be considered important enough to justify being included.
(b) Meaningful: the action must have some cultural meaning for the readership. If they have no knowledge of the significance of an event in a particular culture, then it cannot be included.
(c) Personality: ideally, stories ought to have a clash of personalities or an interesting central figure.
(d) Simple: the event should be very clear and not require any great depth of explanation.
(e) Shock value or sensational: the event should be something out of the ordinary.
(f) Composition: journalists believe that there should be a mix of different types of news in newspapers. Therefore, there will always be a mixture of types of news story.

**Fig. 3** Newspaper readership by social class

**Who reads what?**

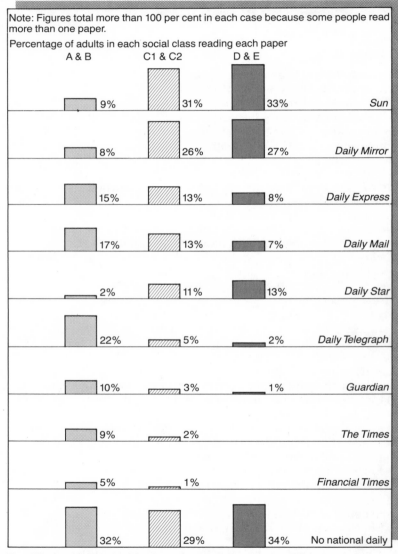

Note: Figures total more than 100 per cent in each case because some people read more than one paper.

Percentage of adults in each social class reading each paper

| A & B | C1 & C2 | D & E | |
|---|---|---|---|
| 9% | 31% | 33% | Sun |
| 8% | 26% | 27% | Daily Mirror |
| 15% | 13% | 8% | Daily Express |
| 17% | 13% | 7% | Daily Mail |
| 2% | 11% | 13% | Daily Star |
| 22% | 5% | 2% | Daily Telegraph |
| 10% | 3% | 1% | Guardian |
| 9% | 2% | | The Times |
| 5% | 1% | | Financial Times |
| 32% | 29% | 34% | No national daily |

The different class readership of newspapers helps to explain differences in their contents.

Source: JICNARS, 1986

## The record industry

The type of popular music which is broadcast and promoted is usually the result of the commercial interests of large record companies.

1  A wide variety of musical types, at any one time, is discouraged. This allows the record companies to operate more profitably.
2  'Safe' and predictable types of music tend to be promoted.
3  As an example of the above, the original radical music of punk groups such as the Sex Pistols was repackaged to make it acceptable to more people and so to sell well.

## Summary

1  The mass media developed with modern technology. Their most significant characteristic is that they are one way. People cannot talk back to them.
2  The mass media provide us with our ideas about the world and so are very powerful when it comes to labelling groups, such as the young, women, etc.
3  There is disagreement over the extent to which the media influence our behaviour. The best explanation is that they reinforce attitudes already held.
4  There is little evidence to prove that people are influenced to commit crimes of violence, etc. by the contents of the media.
5  The media are owned by only a few companies.
6  The contents of the newspapers are a reflection of the type of readership aimed at, the need to attract advertising, journalistic practices and the interests of the owners.

## Revision questions

1  Explain how the communication of the mass media is different from face-to-face interaction.
2  Give an example of the power of the media in labelling a group and creating stereotypes.
3  Briefly state the three explanations of how the mass media influence us.
4  Does ownership of a newspaper by a person or company automatically mean that the contents of the newspaper reflect only their opinions?
5  What two types of newspaper are there?
6  What is meant by the term 'journalistic values'? Give examples to illustrate your answer.

# 14 Poverty and the Welfare State

## Aims of the chapter

In this chapter we will examine:

**1** The different definitions of poverty – in particular the differences between the relative and absolute definitions.
**2** Which groups are likely to be in poverty.
**3** The causes of poverty.
**4** Why those in poverty become trapped there.
**5** The methods of combating poverty.
**6** The origins of the Welfare State.
**7** The debate on the Welfare State between those who argue for universal benefits, and those who support selective benefits.
**8** The services performed by voluntary organizations.

### What is poverty?

There are two definitions of poverty: **absolute poverty** and **relative poverty**.

*Absolute poverty*
According to this definition, poverty is the condition of a person who has not got enough money to feed, clothe and house him/herself adequately. It was first used by a researcher, Joseph Rowntree, in his studies of poverty beween 1899 and 1950. Rowntree said that food, clothing and housing were essentials which everyone needs. He then found out just how much income was needed for a person to remain healthy, to clothe him/herself with the fewest clothes possible in order to stay warm and dry, and to pay for somewhere to live. This level of income he termed the **poverty line**.
There are some problems with this definition:
**1** He expected the poor always to find the cheapest sorts of food that would provide health. Yet people do not always have a sufficient knowledge of diet to choose the cheapest good food.
**2** The cheapest food is usually sold in large portions, which the poor cannot afford.
**3** Rowntree did not allow the poor any 'luxuries' at all (such as cigarettes, entertainment, etc.).
**4** Most importantly, Rowntree failed to realize that what people consider as poverty varies over time.
**5** There was no provision for fashion in the amount allowed for clothes.

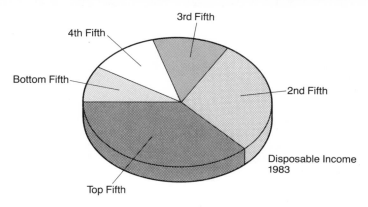

The rich get richer and the poor get poorer:
who has what percentage of the country's
income?

Source: *Central Statistical Office*, 1983 (HMSO)

### *Relative poverty*

The second approach defines poverty directly in relation to
normal expectations of typical people in any society, so poverty
varies over:

**1 · Time** Having a video ten years ago was considered a luxury;
today it is very common.

**2 Society** In the USA and Europe, car-ownership is considered
normal; in most of Africa, it is a sign of great wealth.

This means that it is impossible to draw any clear line between
those in poverty and the rest of the population.

### *How poverty is measured in sociological surveys*

Most people now accept the relative definition of poverty; the
problem remains how to use this in research to measure the
extent of poverty in Britain. The result has been to use the
**supplementary benefits** line, which it is presumed is the
minimum that the Government feels that it can allow people's
income to fall to.

### The significance of different definitions of poverty

These different definitions are important, because they give very
different estimates of poverty. Measuring poverty in absolute
terms would suggest, in this country, that very few people are in
poverty. Measuring poverty in relative terms, however, based on
the claiming of supplementary benefit as the criterion, gives a
total of over 11 million people living in poverty.

Groups in poverty

The following groups comprise the poor in Britain:
1  The low paid.
2  The unemployed.
3  The elderly.
4  The sick and disabled.
5  Single parents.
There is greater poverty in the north of Britain than in the south-east.

**The low paid**  Forty per cent of all families in poverty have a head of household in full-time employment. Some 2.75 million heads of poverty-stricken households are employed, which disproves the idea that the poor are lazy.

**The unemployed**  About one third of the poor consist of the unemployed. There are about 3 million unemployed, though not all are in poverty.

**The elderly**  These account for about 20 per cent of the poor. The numbers of the elderly have increased greatly in recent years. Their pension level is low and they have many extra costs because they normally stay indoors all day. This increases heating and lighting costs, for example.

**The sick and disabled**  A third of the poor are sick or disabled. They either cannot find work or can find only low-paid work.

**Single-parent families**  These are generally headed by a woman. Over half of families with only one parent are in poverty.

**Geographical location**  Poverty and unemployment are more common in the north than the south-east of Britain, as this is where industry has declined the most in recent years.

**K** ▶ The causes of poverty

*The cycle of deprivation*
People born into large families with low incomes, living in bad housing, in deprived inner-city areas, who suffer disadvantage from birth are likely to fail at school. As a result, they are less likely to be able to find work. Any work that is available will be low paid. The result is that they will remain living in the same deprived inner-city area and they will therefore live in poverty. When they have children, they too will be trapped in poverty. The cycle will continue.

*The culture of poverty*
When generations are trapped in poverty, as described above, then eventually they will develop special values and forms of

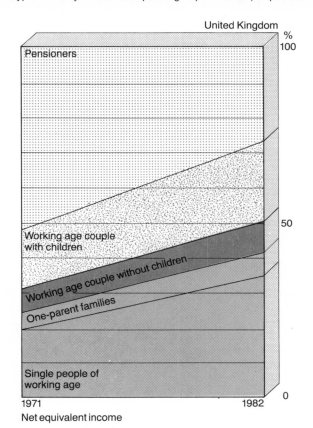

United Kingdom

Source: *Department of Health and Social Security* 1986 (HMSO)

behaviour to cope with life. This has been called the 'culture of poverty'. The special values which the poor develop, such as not caring about the future, not saving any money they earn, seeking as much pleasure as they can get, etc., may well help them to cope with life, but it also ensures that they are trapped in poverty forever. Of course, this does not explain why the poor are poor in the first place.

*Differences in power*
The groups mentioned earlier have very little power. In the competition for jobs and government resources, these groups tend to lose out; the result is poverty. So, the poor are rarely union members or from the middle class. It has been pointed out that the rest of society benefits from their low pay, as many of the most menial jobs are done by the poor.

Living in poverty: the poverty trap

People in poverty do not suffer just from low incomes, they face a wide range of other problems as well.

1  There are fewer doctors in the poorer, inner-city areas, so medical help is harder to find.

2  Studies indicate that the poor are less likely than other groups to use the medical and social services open to them.

3  The children of the poor do less well at school, as they are less likely to get parental encouragement and they suffer from worse home environments. This leads, in turn, to the worst jobs.

4  They are less likely to know their rights to State benefits. For example, there are half a million people who are eligible for supplementary benefits, but do not claim them.

5  The poor often live in the most deprived neighbourhoods, with high levels of pollution, poor-quality housing, older schools and fewer parks or open spaces. Crime rates in these areas are particularly high.

6  As the supermarkets increasingly move out of the towns into the suburbs, the chances of buying cheaper goods are denied to the poor. They have to shop instead at the small local shops, which charge higher prices. Not only that, but limited incomes mean that the poor must buy in smaller amounts, which usually cost more than larger economy-sized packs and jars. The result is that the poor are trapped in their poverty.

 Combating poverty

There are various ways in which poverty is being combated:

1  The National Health Service: provides health, educational and welfare services.

2  Voluntary organizations: provide additional services, varying from the Salvation Army to Shelter (the organization for the homeless).

3  Taxation: the less you earn, the lower the amount paid in taxation.

The Welfare State

*Origins*
The Welfare State had its origins in reforms by the Liberal Government in 1911. However, the system as we know it began with the 1945 Labour Government. That Government said that in future nobody would be permitted to live in poverty and everyone was to have health care based upon need, not money. Finally,

education was to be a right for all children. The Welfare State was to look after its citizens 'from the cradle to the grave'.

The debate over the Welfare State

*Critics of the Welfare State*
In recent years a number of people have begun to question the need for the Welfare State.
▶ **1 Wasteful** They argue that the Welfare State is wasteful, because it gives out **universal** benefits (benefits to everybody), including those who could afford to pay. It would be better to restrict the Welfare State services (such as health) to those who cannot afford to pay privately (e.g. for private medicine). This is known as **selective** provision.
▶ **2 Selectivity** Critics claim that by being selective and giving benefits only to those who need them:
(a) The standards of benefit could be higher.
(b) Taxes could be lowered.
(c) People could therefore afford to pay privately.
**3 Choice** At present, the critics argue people have no choice. They are sent to a particular hospital or a limited range of schools. Payment would give people choice of doctors, schools, hospitals, etc.
**4 Self reliance** The provision of services by the Welfare State robs people of their desire to stand on their own two feet.
   There are also critics from the left, who argue that the Welfare State does not provide adequate services, and that more money ought to be spent and better services provided for more people.
▶    Defenders of the Welfare State argue:
**1** It has eliminated most of the worst poverty, homelessness and chronic bad health.
**2** Without it, the less well-off would be deprived of decent health, educational and housing services.
**3** It is very difficult to isolate the people who desperately need help and it is better to give to as many people as possible.
**4** The Welfare State is remarkably good value for money and is cheaper and better than commercial alternatives.
**5** The people who wish to dismantle the Welfare State are really only looking after their own interests in wanting to lower taxes.

Voluntary organizations

Apart from the services provided by the State, many are provided by voluntary organizations. These are usually charities, which rely on people to work without payment. They fall into two groups:

**1 Charities which help others** These include: Citizens' Advice Bureaux which give advice and help to anyone with legal or official problems; War on Want, which collects money for aid to the Third World; and Shelter, which helps those with housing problems.

**2 Self-help groups** These include: Gingerbread, which helps single-parent families and Alcoholics Anonymous, in which alcoholics help each other with their drinking problems.

Voluntary services are important because:

1 Small voluntary agencies can often cope better with some specific problems, which the State bureaucracy may find difficult to handle. Release, which helps people with drug problems, is an example of this, as is the Terence Higgins Trust, which helps people with Aids.

2 Volunteers are often more flexible in the hours they are prepared to work. The Samaritans have a 24-hour telephone service, for example.

3 Volunteers have often had similar problems themselves and so can bring their own insight into play. Alcoholics Anonymous is run by former alcoholics.

4 Voluntary agencies often exist in order to attack government complacency and inadequate facilities. Clearly, the State could not criticize itself.

## Summary

1 There are two main definitions of poverty: absolute and relative.

2 In sociological surveys, researchers usually use the supplementary benefits line to measure poverty.

3 The different definitions of poverty give very different numbers of people in poverty.

4 The poorest groups in the population are: the low paid; the unemployed; the elderly; the sick and disabled; and single-parent families.

5 There is greater poverty in the north of Britain.

6 The causes of poverty include: the cycle of deprivation; the 'culture of poverty'; differences in power.

7 Living in poverty means more than not having any money. It often means lacking medical services, not benefiting fully from education, etc.

8 Often people are trapped in poverty and are unable to escape.

9 There are various ways to combat poverty. These include the

Welfare State and voluntary organizations.
**10** There is a debate over the future of the Welfare State, between those who argue for universal benefits and those who argue for selective benefits.
**11** Voluntary groups provide services the State is unable or unwilling to provide.

## Revision questions

**1** Explain the main difference between absolute and relative definitions of poverty.
**2** How is poverty usually measured in sociological surveys?
**3** Name any three groups in poverty.
**4** What do sociologists mean by the cycle of deprivation?
**5** Why do people find it difficult to escape from poverty?
**6** Explain the terms universal and selective benefits.
**7** Why do voluntary organizations continue to exist, when there is a Welfare State?

# 15 Urbanization and community

## Aims of the chapter

In this chapter we will examine:

**1** The meaning of the terms urbanization, de-urbanization and rural.
**2** The relationship between urbanization and industrialization.
**3** The relationship between de-urbanization and industrialization.
**4** The differences between life in the cities and life in the countryside.
**5** The meaning of the terms community and association.
**6** The existence of housing zones in the city, and particularly the zone of transition.
**7** The problems of the inner cities.
**8** The causes of the inner-city riots.
**9** The changes in the countryside.

**Urban** is a word which refers to towns and cities. **Urbanization** is the process by which cities grow and the majority of the population moves from the countryside into the cities. Britain was one of the first countries in the world to undergo urbanization. This happened in the 19th century and was very closely linked to industrialization. All the big, industrialized nations in the world have a majority of people living in towns and cities. In the Third World, the process of urbanization is happening now.

**De-urbanization** is the process whereby people start to move out of the towns and cities in large numbers in order to live in the countryside and outer suburbs. This has been happening in Britain for the last 20 years.

**Rural** refers to life in the countryside.

### The relationship between urbanization and industrialization

There is a very close link between industrialization and urbanization. In Britain, during the 18th century:
**1** Changes in agriculture: large landowners drove many of the peasants from the land, who were forced to move to seek work.
**2** Industry: factories with mass production machinery were built, and these needed a large workforce. This attracted people. Houses were needed and these were built around the factories.
**3** Large numbers of people attracted traders.
**4** As towns developed, divisions in areas between the social classes (and much later, ethnic groups) developed. The more affluent originally lived in the city centres, but gradually they moved out to certain suburbs.

In the Third World today:
**1** Manufacturers have switched much production to the poorer Third World nations of Southern America and the Far East.
**2** People have been drawn to the towns in search of employment. This process has been very rapid.
**3** There has been little town planning, or attempt to provide decent housing for the new immigrants from the countryside. So large 'shantytown' areas have developed.
**4** There are tremendous social problems and wide divisions between rich and poor in most Third World cities.
**5** Third World cities are exploding, in terms of population.

### The relationship between de-urbanization and industrialization

In Britain there has been a move away from living in the cities,

since the 1960s. Reasons include:
1  The development of fast means of transport to allow commuting, such as motorways, electrified railway lines, etc.
2  The choice of many companies to move to new 'green-field' sites in out-of-town locations:
(a) Rates and purchase prices are lower.
(b) Communications are often better (no inner-city traffic jams).
(c) People prefer working out-of-town.
3  Houses are pleasanter and often cheaper in the countryside.
4  In the 1960s there was a deliberate attempt by local councils and the Government to encourage people to move out of the cities into new towns and overspill estates.
5  The inner cities have increasingly become places of social deprivation and high crime, so that people are afraid of living there.

**Fig. 1**  Where people are moving (1981 – 4)

| Top losers | %/year | Top Gainers | %/year |
|---|---|---|---|
| Inner London | −0.8 | Dorset | 1.5 |
| Cleveland | −0.8 | East Sussex | 1.3 |
| Merseyside | −0.7 | Isle of Wight | 1.3 |
| West Glamorgan | −0.6 | Cornwall | 1.2 |
| Mid-Glamorgan | −0.6 | West Sussex | 1.1 |
| West Midlands | −0.6 | Somerset | 0.9 |
| Greater Manchester | −0.5 | North Yorkshire | 0.9 |
| Gwent | −0.5 | Buckinghamshire | 0.8 |
| Durham | −0.4 | Cambridgeshire | 0.7 |
| Tyne and Wear | −0.4 | Norfolk | 0.7 |
| South Yorkshire | −0.3 | Suffolk | 0.7 |
| Humberside | −0.3 | Devon | 0.7 |

Source: *New Society,* 1987

**Fig. 2**  Europe's suburbanization and de-urbanization

| | 1970-80 | | 1975-80 | |
|---|---|---|---|---|
| | Suburb-anizing | De-urb-anizing | Suburb-anizing | De-urb-anizing |
| United Kingdom | 42 | 21 | 31 | 30 |
| West Germany | 33 | 14 | 19 | 27 |
| Italy | 50 | 15 | 41 | 23 |
| Benelux | 32 | 2 | 31 | 4 |
| France | 50 | 2 | 57 | 7 |

Source : *New Society,* 1987

### The differences between urban and rural life

The first set of differences are the obvious ones:
1  There is more pollution, noise and traffic in the cities.
2  There is a greater density of population and of housing in the cities.
3  There are far more shops and services available in the cities.

 ### Community and association

Some sociologists have suggested that urban life is based upon **association**, and rural life is based upon **community**.

*Community*
This is generally found in the countryside. 'Community' describes a form of social life in which:
1  People know each other and meet on a face-to-face basis.
2  People feel they have interests in common.
3  People feel attached to a place and identify with it.
4  People are likely to know one another's backgrounds and to be treated differently according to this knowledge.
5  People have **multiple roles**. This means that people are known to each other in a number of different roles. The teacher in the local primary school may also be a neighbour and a fellow member of the local swimming club, etc. This form of social life has also been called **mechanical** society (nothing to do with machines).

*Association*
This is generally found in the city. 'Association' describes a form of social life in which:
1  People do not know many of the people they encounter in daily life.
2  Relationships are impersonal.
3  People do not feel they have many interests in common with others.
4  People do not feel they belong to the area, and they are transient, in the sense that they move from one area to another and from one job to another.
5  People do not know a person's background and so they treat them according to how they behave.
6  People know each other only in particular roles. So, the teacher is not known to parents apart from at the school.
This form of social life is also known as **organic** society.

*Reasons for these differences*
The reasons for these differences are:
1  Size: cities have a huge number of houses and streets. It is easy for people to live a great distance away from each other and so to never meet, except at work.
2  Density of population: the large numbers of people in cities, often in the millions, means that life is more impersonal. It is simply impossible to know large numbers of people.
3  Social differences: there are great differences between the people who live in cities – in income, social class, ethnic group. This can make them interesting places to live, but also creates some tensions.

*Are communities only found in villages in the countryside?*
The idea that communities are only found in rural areas has been strongly criticized by sociologists. In cities, people are aware of neighbourhoods, which have boundaries in people's minds. Within these neighbourhoods it appears that communities do flourish. People feel that they belong, and they may know local shopkeepers and others in the neighbourhood very well. In the countryside, there are divisions too. Just because people know each other, does not mean that they like each other.

## Housing zones

In the 1920s and 1930s in Chicago, sociologists conducted a number of studies to find out about crime rates in the city. As a result of their studies, they found that the city could be divided into quite clear zones. In these zones, there were great differences in style of life, in crime rates and in the groups who lived there. They suggested that the zones took the shape of concentric rings, moving outward from the city centre and growing ever larger:
1  Zone 1 = the business and shopping district.
2  Zone 2 = the older residential districts of large houses. Originally these were built for the rich, but they decay and become divided into flats. This is a run-down, poor area.
3  Zone 3 = this is the stable inner-city working-class area.
4  Zone 4 = this is the typical suburban area of the middle class.
5  Zone 5 = this is the wealthy outer suburban district.
Zone 2 was called the **zone of transition**, and had the highest rates of all social problems. In modern London, this would be the areas of Brixton and Dalston.
   The original Chicago sociologists argued that it was in this zone that immigrants first come to settle, because they cannot

find accommodation anywhere else. The more successful manage
to escape to the better areas of the city. Other groups come and
the successful escape. This constant flow led the zone to be called
the zone of transition. Only the poorest and least successful stay.
This zone, being the cheapest and most run-down, attracts the
poorest and most deprived groups in the population and,
therefore, many of the worst social problems exist here.

This model has some problems. In particular:
1 There has been a move into the inner-city areas by the better
off. They have refurbished these areas – this has been called
**gentrification**.
2 Many of the working class have moved out of the inner-city
areas through local council rehousing programmes, and now live
in large overspill estates.

### K ▶ Inner-city problems

1 Housing: the inner cities have some of the worst housing in
Britain. The redevelopment of the 1960s, when tower blocks and
estates were built, did not solve these problems but made them
worse.
2 Unemployment: the inner cities have at least twice the average
unemployment rate. The jobs that do exist are mainly low paid.
3 Crime rates: the inner cities have the highest crime rates, and
some of the toughest policing in the country.
4 Racial tension: the problems of deprivation fuel the racial
tensions that exist in the inner cities, as there are the greatest
concentrations of ethnic minorities there.
5 Decline: the problems of the inner city reflect the decline of
Britain as a manufacturing nation and the shift of companies out
of cities. There is little likelihood of the situation improving.

*The inner-city riots*
Between 1981 and 1986, there were several inner-city riots, in
which there were pitched battles between the police and some
sections of the local communities. The initial reason was
different in each case. However, the general causes included:
1 Deprivation and poverty: people felt they were more deprived
than the bulk of the population.
2 High unemployment, especially among the young.
3 Racial tension: there are feelings of considerable distrust
between certain groups.
4 'Repressive' policing: certain groups – particularly West
Indians – felt that they were being 'picked-on' by the police.

Rural areas

The de-urbanization of Britain has had considerable effects on the countryside. These include:
1  The decline of the amount of 'unspoilt' rural Britain. There has been a large amount of building in the countryside within reach of the big cities.
2  This has resulted in the growth of **conurbations**, which are cities and towns linked by new housing developments.
3  The move of large numbers of people into the villages and small towns of Britain has destroyed some communities.
4  The purchase of houses in certain villages by commuters has led to their becoming too expensive for less-well-paid locals.
5  There has been a growth in the purchase of second-homes by the better off. This has also raised the price of homes in the country.
6  Where there have been new towns or similar large developments, the local communities have been overwhelmed and destroyed. This happened at Basildon and Milton Keynes.
7  However, the shift of companies into the countryside has brought employment and a raising of wages.

## Summary

1  Urbanization refers to the growth of cities and the movement of the population to live there.
2  De-urbanization is the process whereby people move out of the cities and live in smaller towns or country areas.
3  In most of the world, urbanization was closely linked to the growth of industry, and de-urbanization is linked to major changes in industry.
4  Some sociologists have argued that lifestyles in the city are very different from those in the country. They claim that the country lifestyle is best described as community and the lifestyle of the cities is best described as association.
5  Other sociologists disagree and say that there is a community style of life in the cities, and point to the existence of neighbourhoods.
6  There are certain zones in the city which are clearly distinguishable. One particular zone, called the zone of transition, has most social problems.
7  Inner-city areas are faced with major problems and some are decaying badly.
8  There have been a number of inner-city riots, which are

caused by the long-term build-up of problems in the inner cities.
**9** Rural refers to the countryside.
**10** There have been various changes in the countryside, mainly
due to the way that people and firms have moved out of the cities
to live there.


## Revision questions

**1** Explain the relationship between urbanization and
industrialization.
**2** Why has de-urbanization taken place?
**3** Give three differences in the social relationships between
cities and the countryside.
**4** Are communities found only in the countryside? Explain your
answer.
**5** What is the zone of transition?
**6** Give any three problems faced by the inner-cities today.
**7** Give any three reasons for the inner-city riots of the 1980s.
**8** Give four examples of change in the countryside in recent
years.


# 16  Religion


## Aims of the chapter

In this chapter we will examine:

**1** The importance of religion for social control.
**2** The meaning and extent of secularization.
**3** The growth of non-Christian religions in Britain.
**4** The importance of religion in other societies.

### Religion and social control

Religion plays an important part in showing people the accepted
ways to behave in most societies. It does this by providing a series
of moral rules. The rules are seen as being not simply the rules of
society, but of God. Even though the influence of religion has
declined in Britain today, most of our patterns of behaviour are

based upon Christian religious values.

In the 19th century, Karl Marx wrote that religion was the 'opium of the people'. By this he meant that it was like a drug which clouded their perception of the real world and prevented people seeing just how they were being exploited by the rich. Religion allowed people to accept the wealth of the rich and the fact that other people passed their lives in factories and offices working to continue making them rich. For Marx, religion stopped any revolutionary change, by saying that the rich were rich because that was how God intended it – to change society would be against God's wishes.

Many people have pointed out that religion can bring about great change and can be used to attack the society as it is. An example of the revolutionary power of religion is the revolution in Iran in the early 1980s, when the teachings of Islam were used to attack the government of the Shah of Persia.

*Types of religious organizations*
**1 Churches** are large organizations which tend to be traditional in their teachings on morality and values. Examples include the Church of England and the Roman Catholic Church.
**2 Sects**: these are smaller in membership than churches, strict in their teachings and often have very radical values. Examples include the 'Moonies' and the Jehovah's Witnesses.
**3 Denominations** are larger, more conformist versions of sects which are on their way to becoming churches. They rarely draw such a clear distinction between the clergy and the ordinary church-goer as the churches do. Examples include the Presbyterians and Baptists.

## Secularization

**Secularization** means the decline in the influence and importance of religion in society. There is a great debate over the extent to which the influence of religion has declined.

*In support of secularization*
**1** Church attendances have declined; only 11 per cent of the population attend church regularly.
**2** The number of baptisms and the number of church weddings have declined.
**3** The influence of the church on political and social matters has declined. For example, many practising Catholics ignore the teachings of the church on birth control.

*Criticism of secularization*
**1**  Although there has been a decline in church attendance, there is still a widespread belief in God.
**2**  Attendances at the newer churches and sects have grown considerably.
**3**  Although there has been a decline in attendance overall in Christian churches, there has been a doubling of membership of the Muslim, Sikh and Hindu religions in Britain (reflecting the effect of immigration from the Indian subcontinent).

*Reasons for the growth of denominations and sects*
While the churches have had reduced attendances, the sects and denominations have grown. Reasons for this include:
**1**  The churches have failed to provide clear moral leadership, but have altered their teachings to fit into new values. People searching for alternative values cannot find them in the churches.
**2**  The churches have moved too far away from the working class, the poor and the Christian ethnic minorities, and so have lost touch with them.

*Reason for the growth of non-Christian religions*
The great growth in non-Christian religions reflects the increased numbers of people in the ethnic minorities, who have brought their own faiths with them. In particular, the Muslim, Sikh and Hindu faiths have been brought over by immigrants.

*The importance of religion in a simple society*
In simple societies, such as amongst the Trobriand Islands of the Pacific 60 years ago:
**1**  The 'glue' that held society together was religion.
**2**  Religion helped to explain 'the unpredictable' and gave life meaning. For example, amongst the Trobriand Islanders, there were special rituals to be performed which would ensure that fishing would be good. If the fishing was not good, then the blame lay with the fact that the rituals had not been performed properly.
**3**  Religion marked the seasons, which is especially important in agricultural and fishing societies such as that of the Trobriand Islands.
**4**  Religious ceremonies marked the changes in people's lives – from childhood to adulthood, marriage, etc.

## Summary

1 Traditionally, religion played an important part in social control. It is less important now.
2 There is a debate about the extent to which Britain is becoming less religious.
3 The process by which religion is less influential in society is known as secularization.
4 There has been a large growth in non-Christian religions in Britain. This is the result of immigrants settling here and bringing their own religions with them.

## Revision questions

1 How does religion enforce social control?
2 Church attendances have declined considerably in Britain. What reasons can you suggest?
3 How can it be argued that religion is still important?
4 What non-Christian religions have grown in Britain in the last 20 years? Why?
5 Give an example of the importance of religion in a 'simple' society.

# 17 Methods

## Aims of the chapter

In this chapter we will examine:

1 The methods used by sociologists in research on social life.
2 The meaning, use and variety of sampling.
3 The meaning, use and variety of surveys.
4 How questionnaires are devised and the pitfalls for the researcher.
5 How interviews are devised and the pitfalls for the researcher.
6 Why sociologists rarely use experiments.
7 The meaning and uses of secondary sources.
8 Why some sociologists prefer observational methods.
9 The problems of researchers' values affecting their researches.

In order to make unbiased statements about social life, sociologists are careful to use special methods which ensure accuracy. Sociologists tend to fall into one of two broad groups:

1 Those who believe that an adapted version of the methods used by the physical sciences (such as Physics and Chemistry) ought to be used in sociological research – **scientific** Sociology.

2 Those who believe that, as people are so different from the subject matter studied of Physics and Chemistry, completely different methods are appropriate – **subjective** Sociology.

THE EQUIPMENT IS TO DISPROVE THE THEORY THAT GOD LEFT MINUTE PARTICLES OF MEAT IN THE CANTEEN SAUSAGES

**Fig. 1** The point of studying sociological research methods is to make sure that the most appropriate techniques are used (*Cartoonist: Nigel Paige*)

## Scientific Sociology

This approach begins by organizing any piece of research, in a number of stages:

1 Identifying a particular area of interest.
2 Suggesting a possible explanation – a **hypothesis**.
3 Planning the research.
4 Collecting the information.
5 Analysing the information, once collected.

**6** Comparing and checking the results against the original hypothesis.
**7** Writing a report of the study, with all the conclusions.

The following example, from *The Deferential Worker* (published in 1977) by Howard Newby, shows this process:

**1** He noticed that farmworkers, although extremely lowly paid, showed no anger towards the farmers who employed them.
**2** He thought that they had been brought up to have a special attitude, called **deference**, which meant that they thought farmers were better than them and deserved to have a much higher standard of living.
**3** He decided that the best way to get the information was to collect a list of farms in East Anglia and then to ask farmers and farmworkers a series of questions on their attitudes.
**4** He interviewed a large sample of farmers and farmworkers at their places of work.
**5** He sifted through all the replies, organizing and making sense of them.
**6** He checked his conclusions against his original idea of deference, and found that he had been roughly right.
**7** He wrote a book (*The Deferential Worker*).

## Sampling

Sociologists often want to find out what the whole population thinks about something. Obviously, it would be impossible to ask everybody, so they take a **sample** of people. A sample is a small representative group, who should reflect the characteristics of the whole population.

**Sample frame** This is the source from which the sample is taken. For example, you may wish to find out about people over the age of 18, so you would choose a number of names from the lists of voters kept in every public library.

**Pilot sample** This is a very small sample, chosen before the main research in order to uncover any problems.

**Snowball sample** Sometimes there are special problems getting a sample – for example, if the people you wish to study are engaged in illegal activity. In this case you find one person, gain their confidence and then ask them to give you the names of others.

### Methods by which sociologists ensure samples are representative

There are two main ways by which sociologists ensure that the samples they obtain are typical of the population:

*Random sampling*

This is a way of choosing people to make sure they are typical of the population you wish to study. Quite simply, if you choose people entirely at random, then you have a high chance of getting a typical cross-section of any group. There are three types of random sampling:

**1 Strata sampling** Before you choose people at random, you divide the population into groups, in proportion to their numbers in the population as a whole. For example, you decide that at least 15 per cent of your sample must be over retirement age because you know that 15 per cent of the population in the whole society is over retirement age.

**2 Cluster (or multi-stage) sampling** To save you going all over the country to get your sample, you make sure that you choose certain areas at random and then choose people within these areas – this means that your sample is in clusters, which are easier to obtain results from.

**3 Multi-phase** This is when you do a second, smaller sample after the main one. This helps to check details, or make further in-depth enquiries.

*Quota sampling*

This is when you decide to choose your sample, not by randomness, but by dividing the population into groups on the basis of known facts (age, class, sex, etc.) and then obtain a quota of each group. (It is very similar to strata sampling mentioned earlier, but it has no element of randomness in it.)

K ► Survey types

Once the method of sampling has been decided, the next stage is to decide the type of **survey** to be used. There are three major types:

**1 Cross-sectional studies** This is the type of survey where a cross-section of the population is questioned on issues over a few days. It gives a snapshot view of people.

**2 Case studies** These are sometimes known as in-depth studies: a small group of people, or a particular event (such as a strike), are examined in great detail.

**3 Longitudinal studies** Sometimes sociologists wish to study changes in a group of people over quite a long period of time, for instance, over the whole period of school attendance of a group. This is the complete opposite of the cross-sectional survey.

In the end, the type of survey and sampling method depends

upon what is most appropriate for the sort of information you wish to acquire. There is no 'right' or 'wrong' way.

## Getting information from people

### Questionnaires
These are sets of written questions, which are given out or mailed to people to complete. They are cheap and simply completed, and people can answer embarrassing questions because they are impersonal.

There are certain drawbacks to questionnaires, however: they have to be very simple, otherwise people cannot understand them, and most people do not return them (a low response rate).

### Interviews
These are situations in which people are questioned orally by a researcher. They are useful for understanding complicated issues, and the researcher can ask follow up questions to make better sense of the answers. However, the presence of the interviewer can often influence the answers given (interviewer bias).

### Experiments
These are commonly used by other sciences, but not Sociology. The argument is that people would not behave normally in the special conditions required to make experiments.

### Types of questions
There are basically two types of questions:
1 **Open-ended** Those which leave the person interviewed considerable choice in how they answer the question and which try to uncover complicated ideas. For example, the questions often use the formula: 'What do you think about . . .?
2 **Closed** These are questions where the person interviewed has a limited choice of answers. The interviewer (or questionnaire) really wants specific information, not ideas.

## Secondary sources

Although sociologists often use surveys which they conduct themselves to get information, it is often the case that a survey is impossible. In these cases, the sociologists turn to other published sources of information, and then use these in constructing explanations for behaviour.

**Fig. 2** One set of facts, two stories

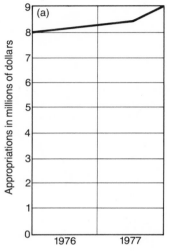
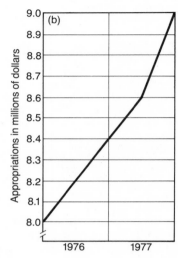

Source: Gomm and McNeil, 1982

The two graphs above are based on exactly the same statistics – they are, however, presented differently. Be careful when you interpret diagrams – they can be made to prove many different things.

There are many types of secondary source: these include:
1 Official government publications and statistics.
2 Statistics collected by other researchers and research organizations.
3 Newspaper reports of events.
4 Historical documents.
5 Novels.
6 Diaries.
7 Parish records.
You can see that the last ones are generally most useful in historical research.

We need to be very careful of uncritical use of secondary sources. Why were the figures collected in the first place? Does this mean that they may be biased? Are diaries and novels reliable, or are they just personal interpretations of events, that may be wrong?

## Subjective Sociology

Earlier we saw that there were two views on obtaining information in Sociology. The first view was that Sociology could be like any other science. These sociologist tend to use surveys and, very occasionally, experiments. On the other hand, there is a large group of sociologists who argue that if sociology is really about understanding people in their environment, then sociologists ought to observe people in their daily lives, and even join in with specific groups. By becoming fully involved in people's lives, sociologists can come to a full understanding of how people see the world, and the reasons for their actions. This is **subjective** Sociology. It is most commonly used when studying delinquent or deviant groups.

The main method used by subjective sociologists is observation. There are two versions of observation. At one extreme, observation can involve merely watching a particular group and having no contact with it – **non-participant observation**. At the other extreme, it can involve the sociologist joining the group and pretending to be one of its members – **participant observation**.

**1 Non-participant observation** The researcher does not get deeply involved with the group under study. This means that he/she does not become biased, but that there may be a shallower understanding of how people behave, as the researcher is not one of them. A big advantage is that the researcher does not influence the actions of the group by his/her presence.

**2 Participant observation** The researcher really gets into the minds of the people under study, by being one of them. This is extremely helpful, but it can lead to the researcher influencing the activities of the group, by his/her presence.

## Research and values

One of the major problems faced by sociologists is that, in studying people and their attitudes, his/her own values may influence what is written. Sociologists must be very careful.

Some sociologists state what their political views are, others try to be as strict as possible concerning any possible bias, and try to elimate any unintentional bringing in of their own values. The best way to overcome the possibility of bias is by being extremely critical of all research. In this way any weak or doubtful ideas are eliminated.

## Summary

1  There is a division between subjective Sociology and scientific Sociology.

2  In order to make statements about society, sociologists often use surveys.

3  In order to ensure that the surveys accurately reflect the views of the population, sociologists use various sampling techniques, particularly quota and random sampling.

4  There are different types of survey; cross-sectional, case studies and longitudinal studies.

5  There are a number of different ways of actually getting information from people. These include questionnaires, interviews, experiments and secondary sources.

6  Each technique of getting information has advantages and disadvantages. But the most important is to try to eliminate any bias that may creep in to studies.

7  Subjective sociologists prefer to join groups and to observe them in action. Sometimes the sociologists pretend to be one of the group. In this case the research is called 'participant observation'.

8  This form of research is especially useful when studying deviants.

9  Sociologists must be extremely careful not to let their own values and prejudices creep into their studies.

## Revision questions

1  What is the difference between scientific Sociology and subjective Sociology?

2  What are the stages of research?

3  Why is sampling important? Why are there different types of sampling? Illustrate your answer with two examples.

4  Explain the meaning of the term 'longitudinal study'? Give an example of when you would use it.

5  What is the difference between an 'open-ended' question and a 'closed' question? Give an example of each.

6  Why are secondary sources useful to sociologists?

7  Give any two problems faced by sociologists doing participant observation.

8  Why should a sociologist's own values cause any difficulty in research?

## 1 Socialization and culture

**1** People learn the accepted way of behaving and the normal beliefs and values of a society.
**2** The example given in the text is Anna. She was unable to walk, to control her bowels, or to understand anything being said to her. However, there are other examples and you could have used any of these. Anna was not really recognizable as 'human' in her behaviour, because she was isolated. This suggests that people must learn to be members of society.
**3** Involved in primary socialization. Children identify with parents. Gender divisions first learned here.
**4** Through the hidden curriculum, in which teachers pass on their own values without necessarily meaning to.
**5** Clearly distinguishable sets of values within the main culture of a society. Any examples you wish. For example – youth styles and fashions.
**6** Patterns of behaviour expected of people occupying a particular social position, for example, a teacher or policeman. Role conflict occurs when a person has two different roles which pull in different directions. For example, the police officer who discovers his/her friend driving with excess alcohol.
**7** Any society you wish, but the one given in the text is that of Samoa in the 1930s. No stress on competition, but great stress on harmony, generosity and kindness.
**8** Norms are the socially expected ways of acting in certain situations. For example, it is a norm to queue in a shop if there are other people waiting to be served, or to shake hands on meeting someone.

## 2 Family and marriage

**1** Result of changing attitudes to marriage by women who are pregnant and not married. Prefer to live alone. Secondly, increase in divorce.
**2** Example given in text is of Indian families. Stress on extended family/close ties/obedience/females under control of males, etc.
**3** Become more equal and women have far greater say. Varies by class. Important to point out women still have to perform most domestic jobs.
**4** Nuclear.
**5** Emotionally intense/women repressed/family violence.
**6** Three of the following: high expectations of marriage;

changing attitudes of women; changing cultural values; legal changes.

**7** Decreased.

**8** Increased rapidly from 1961 to 1972 when it overtook first-time marriages, then declined. However, it still stayed higher than first-time marriages. This can be explained by the high rise in the divorce rate. People are not rejecting marriage, but their partners.

**9** Not true! It shows that women do most of the work in the home and particular jobs done by males.

## 3 Work

**1** Paid; not usually done for pleasure; acceptance of authority; clearly marked off; designed to be productive.

**2** No. They also work for satisfaction; for companionship; a sense of identity; status.

**3** Move away from manual to non-manual work; from manufacturing to service industries; increase in the number of women working; growth in unemployment; growth of multi-nationals.

**4** In the number of factories and machinery; the number of people living in cities; the number of employees working in industry; industrial societies are usually better off; there is a division of labour; plus other ideas you might have.

**5** Can be both good and bad. It can replace boring, dangerous work; produce cheaper goods. It could make people unemployed; as a result could lead to crime/poverty/social unrest. Divisions between the employed and unemployed could grow. Possible political divisions.

**6** Boring, repetitive, low skill levels; little control over the work.

**7** Government action; state of the economy; level of work satisfaction.

**8** It depends on your viewpoint. One group of sociologists argue that trade unions represent the interests of the workers – trying to get higher wages and shorter hours. Professions are meant to maintain a very high standard in certain important jobs such as doctors, etc. However, a second group of sociologists argue that professions just look after the interests of their members and merely create an impression that they are concerned about high standards. Either answer is acceptable, but it is better to show both sides of the argument.

**9** In a non-industrialized society there is no clear distinction between work and leisure; occupations are inherited, not obtained on ability; there is no special time or place reserved for work.
**10** It influences our lives in a wide variety of ways, these include: family relationships/community/leisure/health plus any others you wish to include. Work and travel to work occupies the majority of our time. Our lives are generally built around work.
**11** 15 million.
**12** Intermediate non-manual.

## 4 Unemployment

**1** Decline in manufacturing; foreign competition; automation; economic restructuring.
**2** The young; the old; the ethnic minorities.
**3** Discrimination; greater number of working-class people.
**4** The north has the fastest-declining industries; further away from Europe; less wealth leads to fewer service-industry jobs; financial sector is based in London; new industries developed in the south.
**5** Two from: high costs of unemployment benefits; prevent other forms of investment by governments; weak trade unions and so decline in employees' rights; higher rates of crime; political and social divisions between employed and unemployed. Plus any others you can think of.
**6** To older people, unemployment means loss of status; loss of friends; decline in living standards; possible loss of identity. To younger people, more varied responses. Their identities are less likely to be formed by employment; no salary to lose; fewer financial commitments. But less chance to leave home; to have the lifestyle wanted; to buy car, etc; nothing to look forward to. Plus any extra ideas of your own.
**7** 40 per cent.
**8** The north.

## 5 Social stratification

**1** Three from: infant mortality rates, health, length of life, values, income, housing conditions, plus any reasonable ones of your own.
**2** Because it leads to differences in income and lifestyle. Usually it reflects education.

**3** People from the working class in well-paid, secure employment, who own their own houses in the suburbs. Most commonly found in the south of England.

**4** Differences in pay, prestige, level of skill in job, membership of unions or professions, degree of authority in the workplace.

**5** Bourgeoisie and proletariat. The differences are based upon ownership of property and shares.

**6** Changing occupational structure, educational levels, attitudes to work and promotion, sex, ethnic group and area of the country.

**7** Those who are rich are often from wealthy backgrounds and have connections with other wealthy people. Marriage ties and public school attendance link them to political figures and top civil servants. Those in power will always listen to people who are in charge of large companies employing many people, who could influence the economy of the country.

**8** (a) V.

(b) Health gets worse as class declines.

**9** 20 per cent.

**10** 20 per cent.

## 6 Race

**1** Ethnic minorities are groups of people who share a common culture and who live in a society with a different culture.

Race is a term which is supposed to refer to a group of people who are biologically different from other groups. There are no such things as pure races.

**2** Three from: poverty in the country of origin; persecution in the country of origin; a labour shortage in Britain so immigrants were needed; to join relatives.

**3** They went to cities to find work and then the only accommodation available was in the run-down inner-city areas. They concentrated there as they bought cheap property. New arrivals settled there as there were already people from the same country living there.

**4** Institutional racism is where racist practices are 'built-in' to an organization. For instance, the teaching of history in schools from a European perspective.

**5** When a group is identified as having caused all the problems of a particular society, even though it is untrue.

**6** The three areas in the main text are: employment – worst jobs and low pay; unemployment – have much higher rates of unemployment; housing – have the worst housing; education – do not fulfil their potential; politics – under-represented in the political system.

**7** (a) 34.6 per cent.
(b) 23 per cent.
(c) Whites.

## 7 Gender

**1** Forms of behaviour which are expected from each sex.

**2** Parents expect different behaviour and reward girls for being quiet and gentle; they encourage them to play 'female' games, such as being mum/cooking/looking after dolls; use different language to describe girls; give the children different clothes to wear.

**3** Two from: stricter control in childhood; not fulfilling potential at school; low-paid employment; social life restricted; housewife role.

**4** Three from: increase in the industries which employ women; cheap/flexible labour for employers; women want to escape from restricted home life; fewer children in a shorter period of time.

**5** Greater equality in the home; financial independence; higher income for family; if man unemployed – possible change in roles with man at home looking after children.

**6** Women interrupt their careers to have children; they need to put child care and domestic duties on equal footing with trying to make a career; employers are usually male and less likely to give them promotion.

**7** Work in different types of jobs which are low paid; concentrated in different industries where they receive low pay; more often employed on a part-time basis.

**8** Two from: increase in women working outside the home; fewer children which free women; activities of women's rights pressure groups to change the laws; increased educational opportunities allowing them to compete more equally with men.

**9** Clerical work.

**10** (a) Women.
(b) 27.9 per cent.

## 8 Education

**1** Formal learning consists of the lessons taught in school and college. For example a Sociology class.

Informal learning takes place in casual day-to-day interaction with others. For example, learning to cook from watching and helping parents. (Or any other examples you can think of.)

**2** The ideas and values passed on by teachers in their interaction with pupils. The teacher talks to girls in one way and expects them to act differently to boys. This teaches gender roles. (Or any example you can think of.)

**3** Through its influence on the attitudes to school of the pupil. (You could mention the Willis study or give other examples.)

**4** When people are rewarded and given opportunities solely on the basis of ability or merit.

**5** Slow down the cleverest children; the schools are too large and impersonal; they do not mix children, as they are neighbourhood based.

**6** Three from: stress on skill; new types of examination; YTS; assisted places scheme; city technology colleges. (Or any others you can suggest.)

**7** Three from: differences in parents' treatment; teachers' attitudes and expectations; school timetable; peer group pressure; wider culture; jobs choices/career advice.

**8** No, there are considerable variations. Those of West Indian background and Bangladeshi backgrounds seem to do particularly poorly. Many of those from Indian backgrounds do well. Reasons include: social class; parental encouragement and values; ability with English; levels of discrimination; background culture.

**9** Disadvantaged groups receive extra help. Examples include certain schools in deprived areas receive extra money and resources. (Or an example of your own.)

**10** (a) The higher the class, the greater the number of students at university.

(b) Approximately 20 per cent.

## 9 Social control and crime

**1** Formal control consists of those agencies which exist only to enforce the rules and laws of society. Examples include police, courts, etc.

Informal control consists of the type of social control performed in normal, everyday settings. Examples include family, peer group, etc.

**2** No. Crime means breaking the law. Deviance means actions

which are considered abnormal or wrong by other people.
Deviance includes crime.

3 An act is not deviant naturally. Acts are deviant when other
people consider them so. What is considered deviant varies
according to the situation. An example could be two people
dancing together. OK in a disco, but deviant in a Sociology
examination. (You could give any example at all to illustrate the
point.)

4 Consequences include changing a person's life in some way
according to the label, as is treated differently. Also person sees
him/herself differently so that affects his/her actions. (You could
give specific examples if you wished.)

5 Males are brought up to be more aggressive. Girls more closely
supervised. Girls express rebellion in different ways. Note
criticism of official statistics that they underestimate female
crime.

6 Working class less likely to be successful legally; working-class
subcultures; status frustration.

7 Three from: do not think it is serious; private matter; involve
them in possible prosecution; unaware they are victims of crime;
humiliating. (You could give examples of each of these if you
wished.)

8 'Middle-class' crime which is usually performed by managers/
professionals/companies. Generally involves some kind of
financial or accounting activity. Examples could include:
companies not providing the goods/services they have charged
for; manager could claim too high expenses, etc; food company
selling contaminated meat, etc.

9 (a) 14 – 16.
(b) 5400.

## 10  Politics and power

1 Power is when someone gets another person to do what they
want, by any means whatsoever. Authority is when somebody
does something because they believe the person telling them
what to do has a right to command.

2 Three from: free press; free elections; freedom to criticize the
government; independent police.

3 Three from: social class; geographical location; ethnic group;
age; gender.

4 Because they encourage tactial voting of various kinds.
Typically, people switch votes away from the political party they

support to another party in order to stop a third political party getting into power.

**5** Pressure groups are usually concerned with one issue only: they usually do not try to get representatives elected.

**6** Two from: employment of MPs; publicity; provision of research/information; demonstrations; at the most extreme, illegal methods, such as sabotage.

**7** Pressure groups keep politicians in touch with the people by bringing forward particularly important issues which cut across party lines.

## 11 Population

**1** In order to be able to predict what is going to happen in the future, to allow governments to plan ahead. Examples include: education, housing, town planning, road building, health and social services. (Or any other examples you could think of.)

**2** The birth rate has fallen except for brief periods after World War I, after World War II and in the 1950s.

**3** No. People prefer higher standard of living; change in cultural ideas of the normal-sized family; women's attitudes have changed.

**4** Higher living standards – better diet and housing; better medical care; improvements in public health.

**5** Isolation; poverty; see themselves as a burden on the family. (Plus any other problem you can add from your own experience.)

**6** Possible biological reasons; drink less alcohol; smoke less; less likely to work in dangerous occupations; less likely to die in car/motorbike accidents.

**7** A move towards the south-east and East Anglia. In particular a move away from the north and Scotland. Reasons are connected to the possibility of finding employment.

**8** Just below one million.

**9** It will decline overall.

## 12 Age

**1** People are expected to behave in certain ways according to how old they are. These expectations vary across society. They have little relationship to physical abilities.

**2** No, it is not. The way children are treated varies according to the period of history as well as by society. Examples include the

treatment of children in Victorian Britain, the Ik tribe described by Turnbull, child prostitution in Thailand, gangs in Colombia.
3  It is a ceremony that marks the move from one age group to another. Examples include marriage and retirement in our society (you could use other examples).
4  There is a variety of youth 'cultures' reflecting gender, class and ethnic group, amongst others.
5  Rastas reflect search for status. They go back into West Indian roots for a different culture of their own. Other examples include Teds, Mods, Punks, or any other group you know about and on which you can write.
6  A group against which you measure your own behaviour – usually of your own age.
7  Lack of money to spend on clothes, vehicles, drinking. Possible increase in crime. Club/shop owners aim at older age group with more money. Youth live at home longer and so have clashes with parents. (Plus any more you can think of.)
8  Asians regard them with more respect. More obedient to them. Keep in contact more.

## 13  Mass media

1  The mass media are communications from one source to a large number of people; the audience has little chance to reply; the timetable is pre-arranged; they are normally operated for profit; they use advanced technology.
   Face-to-face interaction is: directly between people; involves an exchange of ideas; no fixed schedule; not generally done for profit; apart from telephone, not done with advanced technology.
2  You could give women, youth, Blacks, homosexuals, political parties, certain nations or any other group. Women are portrayed in two ways: as good mothers or as sexually attractive young ladies. Has consequences for how women are expected to behave.
3  (a) Behaviourist (hypodermic syringe) model – media have a direct influence on people; (b) audience selection: people choose what they want from the media; (c) the cultural approach; media both reflect and create the accepted ideas of a society. They do influence, but in the long term only.
4  No. Other factors are important. They include – need to attract advertisers; need to have a large audience; journalistic values.
5  Tabloids and quality.

**6** Journalists who produce the news have certain ideas about what news ought to be put in to newspapers and how it ought to be presented. Examples include: important/meaningful/ sensational/composition/simplicity, etc. (You could put these into your own words.)

## 14  Poverty and the Welfare State

**1** Absolute definitions try to set a fixed line, based upon the amount of money it takes to survive.

Relative definitions are based on the amount of money it takes to have the things which are regarded as normal in a society.

**2** Usually by supplementary benefit levels (although other relative definitions have been used. You could use any example given in the text.)

**3** Three from: the low paid, the unemployed, the elderly, the sick and disabled, single-parent families.

**4** People born into families in poverty have few chances of escape and so end in poverty themselves as adults.

**5** Lack of power; poor educational chances; have to spend more on buying goods and services; live in areas where there are few jobs; less likely to know their rights; live in deprived neighbourhoods. (Plus any other reasons you can add.)

**6** Universal means everyone is given benefits or assistance. Selective means a test is given to find out those in greatest need. Only these are given the benefits or assistance.

**7** Voluntary organizations fill in the gaps left by the Welfare State; they are often groups which oppose or are critical of the Government.

## 15  Urbanization and community

**1** Industries attracted large numbers of people to live near factories. These attracted traders offering services and shops of various kinds. Modern production techniques produced cars, caused pollution, attracted people from different countries/areas, leading to ethnic mixes. (You could add points of your own to this.)

**2** Crime, pollution, high house prices, traffic congestion forced people out. Firms moved out to new factories on green-field sites that were cheaper, lower rates, etc.

**3** In the countryside it is a community based on: knowing each other; interests in common; attached to a place; ascription; multiple roles, etc. In the towns it is association with the opposite forms of relationship.

4 No. There are also communities in the city. Particularly the areas in which the ethnic minorities live and have formed communities. Also there are working-class communities left. People are aware of neighbourhoods.

5 Inner-city area of large, decaying houses where people first settle when they arrive in the city. The more successful move out. The area has high levels of crime and social problems.

6 Three from: poor housing, unemployment, high crime rates, lack of jobs, racial tension. (Plus any others you wish to add.)

7 Three from: deprivation, high unemployment, racial tension, strict policing. (Plus any others you wish to add.)

8 Increase in numbers of people living there; growth of new towns and commuter houses; increase in factories, etc; change in farming styles with more machines and less employment; plus any other ideas of your own.

## 16 Religion

1 Suggests that social rules are actually made by God. People obey because they believe in God.

2 Decline in belief in God; increasing stress on science and rationality; growth of sects and denominations; churches fail to address themselves to the problems faced by ordinary people; plus any other ideas of your own.

3 Non-Christian religions are increasing in size; growth of sects; people still believe in God, but do not attend church; a large number of people still have their children baptized and marry in churches.

4 Muslim, Sikh, Hindu. Linked to numbers of immigrants and their descendants. (You could also discuss Jewish religion if you wish.)

5 The Trobriand Islanders are given in the main text. You could use any example you know about. In simple societies, religion holds the society together; strengthens the rules and customs; provides explanations for the unpredictable; provides the ceremonies that mark important events.

## 17 Methods

1 Scientific Sociology uses adapted versions of the methods used

by most sciences: surveys and interviews/questionnaires, for example.
2  (a) Identify an area of interest.
(b) Suggest a possible explanation.
(c) Plan the research.
(d) Collect the information.
(e) Analyse the information.
(f) Compare the results against the original hypothesis.
(g) Write a report on the study.
3  It makes sure that the people questioned are typical of the population. If it was inaccurate, then the research would be no use. There are different types of sampling, because conditions may differ from one survey to another and the most appropriate sampling technique must be used.

Cluster sampling saves the researcher travelling over wide distances, for example. Snowball sampling is when the people to be interviewed are hard to find – possibly because they are engaged in deviant activities. (You could have used pilot, random, strata, multi-phase or quota sampling for your examples.)
4  Takes place over a long period of time. For example, following a group of school children throughout their time at school.
5  An open-ended question is one that allows the respondent to say whatever he/she feels like. For example 'What do you think about . . .'?

A closed question forces the respondent into choosing one of a number of replies the interviewer offers him/her. For example, 'How many books on Sociology have you read this year? – None. One. Two. More than two?
6  Provide background material. Useful for historical research. When people cannot be interviewed. Statistical information.
7  Researcher could influence the group under study by his/her presence. Group could influence the viewpoint of the researcher. Plus any other problems you can suggest.
8  Values can ruin research because researcher could adjust findings (consciously or not) to fit in with his/her values.

**1**  When it comes to examination time, do not do too much the night before. It is best to have a relaxing evening and go to bed early. This will ensure you are fresh for the following day.

**2**  Leave home in plenty of time for the examination.

**3**  In the examination room itself, stay calm, read the question paper carefully and answer what the question asks you, not what you would like to be asked. In my experience, the main reasons for people failing examinations are that (a) they do not read the question correctly or (b) they write down everything, on the principle that they must somehow be giving the examiner what he/she wants. Make sure that you answer what you are asked in as clear a manner as possible.

# Index

KU-764-702

# Contents

# Prologue

The footsteps drew nearer.  They were coming.

Nick Hooper could hear two people talking, but couldn't make out what they were saying.

He had nowhere to hide.  There was no one to help him – only the cleaners were left. Smith School had been closed for an hour.

Nick should never have done what he did, but now it was too late.  He had to hide the tape, but where should he put it?

The footsteps sounded louder in the long corridor outside. Nick knew who had sent them and why. He could run for it, but what was the point?

Wait. He had an idea.

Nick tried the door of the big store cupboard at the back of the classroom.

This was where Mr Fisher, the Media Studies teacher, kept all the television and video stuff. The door was unlocked. That was odd. Mr Fisher must have been in a hurry and forgotten to lock it.

Nick turned on the light. There was a row of Video 8 tapes on a high shelf. Nick took one out of its box. He swapped one of the tiny Video 8 cassettes with another from the pocket of his fleece.

Maybe he would get away with it.

Nick heard their voices right outside the classroom door.

Should he stay in the cupboard?

No.  They were bound to find him.

He turned off the light and went back into the classroom.  He hung his fleece on the back of a chair.

As he sat down, the door opened.

# Chapter 1
# Clueless

Detective Inspector Dudden drove into Smith School at 5.11 p.m.

It was early winter and just starting to get dark. The policeman hurried to Mr Fisher's classroom.

Tall, pretty Community Constable Carpenter was waiting in the corridor outside the room.

"I did what you said, sir," she said. "I've locked all three of them in the classroom."

"How old are they?" Inspector Dudden asked.

"They're aged about 15 or 16," the constable replied.

There was a small window in the door. The inspector looked through it.

He saw three youths. Two of them were wearing dark puffa jackets. The other was in shirt sleeves, even though the school heating had been turned off.

All three boys looked shifty, Inspector Dudden thought. One had black hair. One had red hair. The one in shirt sleeves had blonde hair. What were they doing here?

The inspector was sure of one thing. There had been several thefts from this room. One or more of these boys was behind them.

"Have you rung Mr Fisher?" the inspector asked Constable Carpenter. "After all, this is his classroom."

"Yes, sir. But there was nobody home. I left a message on his answering machine, asking him to come in."

"I see," said the inspector. "The trouble is we won't know if anything's missing."

"Unless we find it on them, sir."

"That's true," Inspector Dudden said, "but they've had plenty of time to put things back. Oh well, let's go and have a word with them."

Constable Carpenter unlocked the door.

The room looked like there had been a fight in it. Tables and chairs had been tipped over. There was a blood stain on the teacher's desk.

"Do you know any of these boys?" Inspector Dudden asked Constable Carpenter.

"I'm afraid not, sir," she said. "None of them has been in trouble on my patch."

Inspector Dudden looked carefully at them.

The blonde boy was the tallest. He had crooked teeth and a bloody nose. This did not make him a villain, but it made him look like one.

The red-haired boy had a bruise on his cheek, but that did not make him the victim, either. He could have started a fight, then got hurt himself.

The black-haired boy was the most heavily built. He had a bloody nose, too.
The inspector decided to pick on him first.

He took the boy out into the corridor.

"What's your name?" he asked the ·k-haired boy.

˙ck Hopper," the boy replied.

"Do you go to this school?" the inspector asked.

"Yes, sir," the black-haired boy said.

"And what are you doing here?" Inspector Dudden asked.

"Mr Fisher put me in detention," the youth explained.

"What for?"

"Losing equipment, sir."

"And where is Mr Fisher?" the inspector asked.

"He never showed up, sir," the boy explained. "But I waited here anyway. You don't miss Mr Fisher's detentions. Everyone's terrified of him."

"I see," said the inspector. "And what are these other boys doing here?"

"I don't know, sir. They showed up and started throwing things around. I tried to stop them. The tall lad gave me this nosebleed."

"Do you know who they are?" Inspector Dudden asked.

"No. I don't think they even go to this school!"

"All right. Thank you, Nick."

Next the inspector sent for the red-haired boy with the bruised face.

"What's your name, son?"

The red-haired boy gave him a confident look. "Nick Hopper," he said.

Inspector Dudden looked at Constable Carpenter.

"Things are getting interesting," she said. "This is quite a coincidence, two of you sharing the same name."

# Chapter 2
# Nick Nick

The second Nick Hopper told the same tale as the first one. He was doing a detention when two boys charged in and started a fight.

"Have you any proof of your identity?" Inspector Dudden asked.

"I'm afraid not, sir. I forgot my bag today."

"All right, go back to the classroom and send out the third boy," the inspector said.

"And what about you?" the inspector asked the tall, blonde-haired boy with the crooked teeth and no coat. "Do you have a name?"

"I'd rather not say," the blonde boy said. He looked worried.

"Perhaps you're called Nick Hopper, too," the inspector said, sarcastically.

The boy didn't reply.

He was probably the thief, Inspector Dudden decided. But which of the other two boys was his mate? Or were they both innocent?

They couldn't both be called Nick Hopper, could they?

The inspector turned to Constable Carpenter.

"This puts us in a difficult position," he said. "Before we take them to the station, we really ought to call their parents."

"I agree," Constable Carpenter said. "Perhaps we should see if they have any proof of identity on them."

"Good idea," the inspector said.

The two officers went into the classroom.

The lads sat as far apart from each other as they could.

"All right," the inspector said. "Turn out your pockets."

The black-haired boy did as he was told.

In his pockets he had a penknife, a house key, some scrunched up tissue and one piece of chewing gum. There was nothing with his name on it.

"Now you," Constable Carpenter said to the redhead.

The red-haired boy also emptied out his pockets.

He had some polo mints, a key ring with two keys on it, and a small ballpoint.

Again, there was nothing with his name on it.

"Now you," the inspector said to the blonde boy. "Let's see what you've got on you."

But the blonde boy's trouser pockets were empty.

"Where's your coat?" Constable Carpenter asked him.

"On the back of that chair," the blonde boy said. He pointed at the brown fleece.

Inspector Dudden went over and checked the pockets.

There was no bus pass in it. No keys, either. This boy was a real mystery. But there *was* something.

Was it cigarettes?

"What's this?" he said, pulling out a tiny plastic box.

He looked at the Video 8 tape, hoping that it would be labelled. There was nothing written on it.

"I wonder," the inspector said, "whether we can see what's on this. Where would I find a video player?"

He looked from the first boy to the second boy to the third boy.

Finally, the blonde boy cracked.

"You can play it on one of the video cameras in that store cupboard over there," he said, pointing at a green door.

"How do you know that it's a store cupboard?" Constable Carpenter asked.

"I have lessons in this classroom," the blonde boy said.

"What was your name again?" Constable Carpenter asked, sneakily.

The blonde boy didn't reply.

"Maybe there's a name in your fleece," Constable Carpenter said.

She picked it up and looked inside.

There was no name. However, as she lifted the fleece, she felt something moving about.

It was in the same pocket where the inspector had found the video tape.

"What's this?" she asked.

She pulled out something cold, heavy and metallic. "A magnet!"

Constable Carpenter handed the item to Inspector Dudden.

"I suppose you think you've been very clever," Inspector Dudden said to the blonde boy. "The magnet will have erased whatever was on this tape."

The blonde boy shrugged his shoulders and replied, "Somebody thinks they've been clever."

"And you still won't tell us your name?" Constable Carpenter asked.

"You wouldn't believe me," the blonde boy said.

Constable Carpenter and Inspector Dudden looked at each other.

"Where do we go from here?" the inspector wanted to know.

The three lads sat waiting for their decision.

"Why don't we make them sweat?" the constable whispered to her boss.

"Good idea," the inspector whispered back. Then he added, in a loud voice, "Do any of you want to call your parents to tell them you'll be late?"

None of the boys took up his offer.

"There's only one thing for it," Inspector Dudden told Constable Carpenter. "I'm going to get the headteacher. She can sort this out."

The inspector went to the door.

"Don't let this lot out of your sight," he told Constable Carpenter.

# Chapter 3

# Who's Who?

The three boys sat on the tables in the cold room, not looking at each other.

The real Nick wondered how he was going to get out of this. Constable Carpenter seemed OK. Maybe if he could get her on her own ... but he wasn't sure that he could convince her of the truth. Things were too confusing.

Nick hadn't expected to have his name stolen. That made things more complicated.

The other two boys had tried to beat him up.  They'd warned him that something worse would happen if he didn't hand over the tape.

If Constable Carpenter hadn't arrived in time, Nick would have been badly hurt.
He wanted to tell Constable Carpenter the truth.

But what was the point?  It was safest to wait.

********

Constable Carpenter looked at the three boys. The blonde one with the crooked teeth was chewing his fingernails.

He would be the first to crack, she decided.

"You might as well tell me now," she said. "Inspector Dudden's gone off to fetch somebody who can identify you all."

The black-haired boy (who she thought of as Nick One) looked fed up.

"Isn't it about time you let us go?" he asked. "I'll be late for my tea."

"Give us your phone number and I'll warn your mum," Constable Carpenter told him.

"You've got no right to hold us here," the red-haired boy (Nick Two) said.

"That's as maybe. If you give me your home address, we'll drop you off there in a little while," Constable Carpenter said.

21

"Otherwise, I'll assume that you've got no home to go to. So I'll keep you here for your own protection."

Nick One and Nick Two sneered at her.

*Which of them was the fake?* she wondered. *Why was one pretending to be the other?*

Constable Carpenter wasn't a detective, but she knew a few things about criminals. Most of them were very stupid. A few thought that they were clever. They tended to be even more stupid.

Which of these three boys had set off the alarm in the store cupboard? It was a secret alarm. Even the class teacher, Mr Fisher, didn't know about it.

Only the headteacher and the police knew it was there.

The alarm had been the headteacher's idea. It was connected directly to the police station. The Head, Mrs Roser, was dead keen to find out who kept stealing the school's audio-visual equipment.

Three video recorders, four video cameras and a mixing desk had gone in the last few months. The school's insurance premiums were going sky high.

Who was responsible?

It had to be one of Mr Fisher's Media Studies students. But how had they done it? There had never been any sign of a break-in.

"I've had enough," the red-haired boy said. "I'm going."

"Me too," the black-haired boy said. "You've got no right to hold us."

They both got off their tables and stood in front of Constable Carpenter.

They looked like they were going to barge past her. Constable Carpenter reached out and grabbed both of them by the collars of their jackets.

"You're not going anywhere," she said.

"We might not be," Nick One said. "But he is."

Constable Carpenter looked over his shoulder. The blonde boy had grabbed his fleece from the back of the chair.

"Catch you later!" he shouted, and swerved past her, out of the door.

"Come back!" Constable Carpenter yelled.

*You stupid cow!* she called herself. *Why hadn't she locked the door when the inspector left?*

But it was too late. The blonde boy had gone.

A minute later, Inspector Dudden returned with Mrs Roser.

"Where's the kid with no name?" the inspector asked.

Constable Carpenter, embarrassed, explained what had happened. Mrs Roser was understanding.

"Strictly speaking," she said, "we can't keep anybody after school without their parents' permission. Now, who are these two?"

"We were hoping that you'd be able to tell us that," Inspector Dudden said.

"They don't look very familiar," Mrs Roser said. "What did you say your names were?" she asked the two boys.

"Nick Hopper," they said in chorus.

"And whose class are you in?"

"Mr Fisher's," said the black-haired boy, Nick One.

"And why are you here?" the headteacher asked the second Nick.

"Detention," the red-haired boy said.

"Where's your detention form?" Mrs Roser wanted to know. "Come on, I want to see what Mr Fisher wrote."

"Is that it?" Constable Carpenter said, pointing at a pink form on the teacher's desk.

"Yes." The Head picked it up and read aloud, "*Nick is behind with his coursework and has used the school video equipment without permission.* Which of you would care to explain this?"

Neither boy said anything.

"It would be helpful," Constable Carpenter told Mrs Roser, "if you could tell us which of these boys is the real Nick Hopper."

"I wish I could," the Head said. "But, to be honest, I don't recognise either of them. This is a big school, and ..."

She didn't finish her sentence. Constable Carpenter had another idea.

"Is there a photograph in Nick's file?" she asked.

"Normally, there would be," Mrs Roser said. "I checked Nick Hopper's file before coming over here. The trouble is, he moved here halfway through Year Eight. That was long after the photos were taken. So we only have his home address and phone number."

"Why don't you try ringing his parents?" Inspector Dudden suggested. "They can tell us whether their son has dark hair or ginger hair. Then we'll be a little nearer solving this mystery."

"Good idea," Mrs Roser said. "I'll go and call now."

"While you're at it," Constable Carpenter said, "maybe you could see if Mr Fisher's home yet."

"Of course," Mrs Roser said. "He ought to be able to shed some light on this situation."

She hurried out of the classroom. Inspector Dudden blocked the door.

"Don't either of you even think of trying to run away again," he said.

The two Nicks sat back down on the tables.

They didn't look at each other.

*Nick One seemed angry with Nick Two*, Constable Carpenter thought. *Why was that? Which of them had tried to break into the store cupboard?*

The Head returned.

"There's nobody in at Nick's and Mr Fisher's not back yet," she said.

"You'd better let us go," Nick Two said.

"Yeah, you can't keep us forever," Nick One pointed out.

"Hold on," Constable Carpenter said. "I've got an idea."

# Chapter 4

# The Truth

Ten minutes later, a police car drew up outside Nick Hopper's house. Large lime trees shaded the small semi.

The two boys sat in the back with Inspector Dudden.

"We don't want anyone else running off on us," he said.

The two Nick Hoppers got out of the car. They were whispering to each other.

Constable Carpenter couldn't make out everything they said.

She was pretty sure what the big one was whispering, though.

"It's all your fault," Nick One was telling Nick Two.

Curtains twitched and blinds rustled all along the street. The neighbours wanted to know what the police were doing there.

"Get out your key," Inspector Dudden told Nick One.

"It won't fit," the lad said, angrily.

"Why's that, then?" the inspector asked.

"Because it's the key to my bike lock," Nick One replied. "I don't have a key to the house."

He handed the key to the inspector.

He was right.  It was the wrong kind of key.

"And where's your bike?" the inspector wanted to know.

"Back at the school," Nick One said.

"You'll have a bit of a walk then, won't you?" Constable Carpenter pointed out.  She turned to the other boy.  "All right, let's see your keys!"

Reluctantly, Nick Two put a hand into his pocket.

*He must be the real Nick*, Constable Carpenter decided.  Maybe some of the stolen stuff was inside the house.

Nick Two handed his key ring to Inspector Dudden.

The inspector was fitting a key into the lock when the front door burst open.

"What the ...?" An angry-looking woman was glaring at them. "Who the heck do you think you are?" she demanded. Then she spotted Constable Carpenter.

"I'm sorry," the constable said. "We didn't think that anybody was home."

"So I can see," said Mrs Hopper. "What's going on?"

Inspector Dudden took over. "We need to know one thing," he said. "Which of these boys is your son?"

Mrs Hopper looked confused.

"*My son*!" she said. "Why, neither of them. My Nick's upstairs. He got home ten minutes ago, just after I got back from the childminder's. NICK!" she yelled, "COME DOWN HERE!"

A moment later, they heard footsteps on the stairs.

The tall, blonde boy with crooked teeth appeared in the hallway. He looked embarrassed.

"Looks like we've caught you, my lad," Inspector Dudden said.

"What's going on?" Mrs Hopper wanted to know.

"There's been a bit of a misunderstanding," the real Nick said.

"Why didn't you tell us your real name?" Constable Carpenter asked him.

"Because you wouldn't have believed me, not after these two both pretended to be me," Nick explained.

"I was sitting near the door," the real Nick went on, "so I could hear what they said.

"First they came in and tried to beat me up, then they pretended to be me!"

On the path, Nick One began to kick Nick Two. "This wouldn't have happened if you hadn't copied me!" he said. "Idiot!"

"I didn't hear what you said!" the red-haired boy complained. "I didn't know what game you were playing. Nick Hopper was the only name I could think of!"

"Will someone tell me what this is all about?" Mrs Hopper demanded.

Inspector Dudden explained.

Mrs Hopper turned to the real Nick. "Have you been stealing equipment?" she asked.

"No. Of course not!"

"You had that video camera at the weekend," Mrs Hopper pointed out. "You said you had permission to borrow it."

"I did, from Mr Fisher. Only he didn't know what I really wanted to borrow it for."

"What *did* you want to borrow it for?" Constable Carpenter asked.

"To catch the thieves who've been stealing stuff from our school," Nick explained. "Everybody in our Media Studies class is behind with their work because people keep stealing the equipment."

"And how did you hope to catch them?" Inspector Dudden asked.

"Easy," Nick said. "Everybody knows that dodgy stuff gets sold in the car park of the *Coach and Horses*. So I went and staked it out on Saturday night."

Nick One and Nick Two began to look worried.

"I hung around for hours," the real Nick explained. "Then I saw these two idiots getting electrical gear out of the boot of a car. They handed the stuff over to someone."

"This proves nothing," Nick One said, angrily. "He's making things up."

"I'm not," Nick said. "I videoed it. The film's shadowy, but I'll bet you can make out that it's you two."

"We'll see about that," Inspector Dudden said. "Where's the tape?"

"It's at school," Nick said.

"I think you'll find that someone put a magnet next to it," Constable Carpenter pointed out. "If you remember they were both in your pocket. Magnets distort video tapes. The picture's probably no good."

"I switched the video tapes when I heard these two coming," Nick said. "I went into the storeroom and took a blank tape from there. The original's on the top shelf."

Inspector Dudden grinned and turned to the Head. "It looks like we have the vital evidence, Mrs Roser," he said.

The Head smiled. "It's lucky you went into the storeroom, Nick. You see, we had an alarm installed in there at the weekend. It alerted the police that there was a break-in. That's why they got to you before these two could finish beating you up."

"I was fighting them off pretty well, thank you," Nick said.

"But what I don't understand is this," the Head said, thinking aloud. "Why was the storeroom door open?"

"Mr Fisher left it unlocked," Nick said. "He left the room while I was in detention and never came back."

"But why were you in detention?" the Head asked him.

"Mr Fisher said it was because I was seen in the car park with a video camera. He lent me the camera himself. The condition was that I only used it at home."

"I should hope so, too," said Mrs Roser. "We can't have people taking school equipment to dodgy places where it might be stolen."

Nick frowned. Mrs Roser realised what she'd said and blushed.

"But what happened to Mr Fisher?" Constable Carpenter asked. "Where did he get to?"

"That's what I'd like to know," Nick said.

All five people turned to the two fake Nicks.

"No idea," Nick One said.

"I don't even know what he looks like," Nick Two said.

"That's right," Nick One confirmed. "We don't even go to Smith School."

"Well, you're going back there now," Inspector Dudden said.

# Chapter 5

# Guilty!

All six people squeezed into the police car (Nick's Mum stayed behind because she had to look after his brother and sister). A message came on the police radio.

"There's been another break-in at the school," it said.

They drove into the school car park with sirens blaring. Constable Carpenter had to drag the two fake Nicks along behind her.

When they got to the classroom, it appeared to be empty.  But the door to the video cupboard was open.  There was a rattling noise inside.

"Police!  Come out of there, whoever you are!" called Inspector Dudden.

A man in his mid-twenties appeared from the cupboard.  It was Mr Fisher.  His fierce face now looked sheepish.  He turned from Inspector Dudden to Constable Carpenter to the real Nick to Nick One to Nick Two and finally to Mrs Roser.

"What are you doing back at school?" the Head asked.

"There was a message on my answering machine," Mr Fisher said.  "It sounded like there was a problem."

"Yes," Mrs Roser said.  "There is a problem." She pointed at the two fake Nicks. "Do you know these boys?"

"No," Mr Fisher said. "I've never seen either of them before."

"But you know this boy," she said, pointing at the real Nick.

"Oh yes, I had him in detention."

"Why did you leave him here, unattended?" Mrs Roser asked.

"I didn't," Mr Fisher said. "I told him to go. He can't have heard me."

*That's not true*, Nick thought, but he didn't say anything. He was beginning to suspect what had really happened.

"Why did you leave the video cupboard door unlocked?" Inspector Dudden asked.

"Was it unlocked?" Mr Fisher asked. "If it was, that must have been a mistake," he admitted. "When I got the message on the answering machine, I thought there had been another robbery. That's why I hurried back."

"Is anything missing?" the Head asked.

"Not as far as I can see," Mr Fisher said.

"Good. Please set up a video and TV for us."

"Why?" Mr Fisher asked.

"Just do as I say, please," Mrs Roser said.

Mr Fisher went and got the TV out.

While he was connecting the video camera, Mrs Roser took Nick into the stock cupboard.

"Is the tape still here?" she asked him.

Nick went through the tapes on the top shelf.

"I put it in the box the wrong way round," he told the Head. "So I think this is it."

As the tape went into the machine, the other two boys looked worried. On the telly, there was a dark pub car park. A white Golf

44

had its boot open. Two people were taking things out of it. They looked just like Nick One and Nick Two.

"Freeze frame the picture!" Inspector Dudden said, then cursed. "I can only make out the first two letters of the car's number plate."

Suddenly, Nick realised something. While everybody else was watching the video, he slipped out of the room. Nick hurried to the car park. There were only three cars in it. One was the Head's. One was the police car. The other was a white Golf.

When he got back to the classroom, Inspector Dudden was yelling at the two fake Nicks.

"Which of you stole the stuff? Was it both of you? How did you know to find Nick here, after school? AND WHAT ARE YOUR REAL NAMES?"

But the boys were both silent.

"I think I know what happened," Nick said.

Everybody turned to him.

"These two didn't steal the video equipment," Nick announced. "They don't go to this school. I watched them in the *Coach and Horses* car park. They were selling all sorts – smuggled cigarettes, dodgy perfume, stereo stuff. I reckon that they bought the video equipment from the real thief."

"And who's that?" Mrs Roser asked.

Nick explained. "The real thief told these two thugs that I'd be here. The idea was that they would beat me up and get the tape out of me. The thief drives a white Golf which is in the car park now. The first letters of his number plate are ..."

Before Nick could finish the sentence, Mr Fisher jumped to his feet and began to run.

He didn't get very far. Inspector Dudden stuck his foot out and the teacher went flying. Mr Fisher twisted his ankle as he fell, then banged his head on the wall. The two police officers picked him up.

"I suspected him all along," Mrs Roser said, as Constable Carpenter handcuffed Mr Fisher. "That's why I didn't tell him about the alarm on the video store cupboard. But why did he leave it unlocked? The police wouldn't have come if he'd locked it."

"I reckon he took some more stuff and meant to frame me for the robbery," Nick told her.

"You could be right," Inspector Dudden said. "We'll get a search warrant for his house. Well done, Nick."

"Your mother will be worried," Mrs Roser told Nick. "If the police are finished with us, I'll give you a lift home."

"That's fine," Inspector Dudden said. "We'll take your statements in the morning. But, as for you three ..." He looked at the two fake Nicks and Mr Fisher with a fierce grin, "You're nick-nick-nicked."

# More about the author:
## My Comic Life

I like finding different ways to tell stories.

I write stories for UNICEF – the United Nations Children's Education Fund.  The stories I write are about children's rights.  Everybody likes comics.  They're more like movies than books.  They can tell complex stories about problems like people's rights to have water.

Stories in comics can happen in outer space.  You don't need lots of money for the special effects. All you need is the writers' and artists' imagination.

I write about things I think are important. But publishers turn down a lot of my ideas. They say that young readers don't care. Or, they do care, but they won't buy books. Or they say someone else has already written about it. So we don't need another book about the same thing, do we?

I used to get round this problem by sneaking serious issues into my crime stories. I put the important things I care about into the stories I wrote. The stories always came first and the issues flowed out of them. It's the other way round in my work for UNICEF. The issues come first. I have to find a good story that lets me write about a problem.

I've written a few bestsellers. None of them have reached as many readers as the UNICEF comics. They printed 360,000 copies of their latest comic.  They're used in schools, so each one is read a lot of times.  The UNICEF comics have more readers than any other comics in the world.  And they're given away free.

Comic books got me hooked on reading. Every week my grandparents used to post a bunch of comics to my brother, Paul, and me. They were *The Beano*, *The Dandy*, *Hotspur* and *TV Comic*.

I got through loads of novels by Enid Blyton but comics were my big love.  When I was eight I discovered *Superman* and *Batman*. I spent all my pocket money on them.  A little later, I found Marvel comics.  They were still in their Golden Age of fantastic art and stories.  I became an addict.

*Spiderman* was my favourite.  Then *X-Men*, *The Fantastic Four* and *The Silver Surfer*.  But Marvel comics were hard to find.  No shops in West Kirby where I lived had them every

week.  I found the issue of *Spiderman*
featuring the death of Gwen Stacey one time
when I went on a rare visit to Birkenhead.

Marvel stories were aimed at college kids.
I learnt a lot of big words from them.  But I
thought comics might be a bit babyish.  When
I was 12, I went to grammar school.  People
thought you were stupid if you read comics.
So all the Marvel and DC comics went into an
outhouse next to the garage.  I read the
music papers instead.

One day, Mum put all my comics in the
bin.  I didn't feel too bad at the time.  But
years later, when I collected re-issues, I felt
sad that I'd lost so many.  Some of the comics
that Mum threw away were worth a fortune.
The same thing happened to lots of other
people I know.  So here's some advice.  If you
have a collection that you're not interested in
any more, *don't* throw it away.  Pack it up
well and put it somewhere safe.  If you don't

want it later on, you can always flog it on *ebay*.

My interest in comics started up again when I went to university. There was a terrific new Marvel comic called *Howard The Duck*. Only one shop in Nottingham sold it and that was on the other side of the city from where I lived. Yet I built up a full collection. Then I began to read *Doctor Strange* and a bunch of other comics I used to have when I was a kid. They made a great change from the big long "Classics" I was reading for my teachers.

I still like reading comics. My favourites are *Optic Nerve*, *Stray Bullets* and *Eightball*. I have a huge comic collection and have nearly all the first editions of my favourite, *Love and Rockets*.

About 15 years ago, I tried to write a comic novel. I planned the pictures and story with my old friend, John Clark, who draws cartoons.  It didn't work.  That was before I started writing books.

Twelve years later, John knew I still read comics.  We'd talk about them when we met.  After he'd done a couple of UNICEF comics on his own, he asked if I'd like to have a go at writing one.  I said I'd love to.  But it turned out to be difficult.

The words often come first.  This is normal for me – and most other people.  I tend to read the words before I look at the pictures.  But working out what picture goes in each square of the comic is hard work.  It makes me see what great, exciting work all those early superhero stories were.

But I don't write about superheroes.  I write about children in danger, in the UK and abroad.  The short stories so far are about child abuse and being homeless.  John drew the one I'm most proud of.  It takes up a whole comic and it's called *Cry Me A River*.

It's about globalisation and the fight for water.

Your school (and you) can get the UNICEF comics, too. They're called *All Children Have Rights*. You can get them for free if you ring UNICEF's helpdesk on 0870 606 3377.

You can find out more about children's rights by visiting the UNICEF children's rights site at http://www.therightssite.org.uk/ You can read about how John and I wrote *Cry Me A River* at http://www.brickbats.co.uk/ Unicef%204.html

You can also visit my website and contact me at www.davidbelbin.com

If you loved this book, why don't you read ...

Ship of Ghosts

by Nigel Hinton

ISBN 1-842991-92-2

Mick's desperate to go to sea, just like the dad he never saw. Now he thinks his dreams are coming true at last. But his adventures turn into nightmares as he slowly finds out about a terrible secret ... what did happen on the Ship of Ghosts?

You can order *Ship of Ghosts* directly from our website at **www.barringtonstoke.co.uk**

If you loved this book, why don't you read ...

# Wings

## by James Lovegrove

## ISBN 1-842991-93-0

Az dreams of being like everyone else. In the world of the Airborn that means growing wings. It seems impossible, but with an inventor for a father, who knows?

You can order *Wings* directly from our website at
**www.barringtonstoke.co.uk**

If you loved this book, why don't you read ...

# The Ring of Truth

# by Alan Durant

ISBN 1-842991-91-4

**"If we gave the ring to the police, we were dead ..."**

Ros and Fish find a ring near to where they hang out on the common. When a body is discovered a few days later, they realise it's evidence – vital evidence in a drugs related murder. Ros and Fish know too much. They have to find the killer before the killer finds them.

You can order *Ring of Truth* directly from our website at **www.barringtonstoke.co.uk**

If you loved this book, why
don't you read ...

# Dream On

## by Bali Rai

## ISBN 1-842991-95-7

"If you dream, it must be for real ..."

Baljit's mates knew what was what. If you were good at football, really good, you could go places. But all his old man ever talked about was duty to the family and paying bills. Baljit couldn't just go on working in his old man's chippie. He wanted out!

You can order *Dream On* directly from our website at **www.barringtonstoke.co.uk**